W9-DEK-175

Sex and Isolation

Sex and Isolation

And Other Essays

Bruce Benderson

The University of Wisconsin Press

PROPERTY OF WZU
SOCIAL WORK LIBRARY

DISCARD

The University of Wisconsin Press
1930 Monroe Street, 3rd Floor
Madison, Wisconsin 53711-2059

www.wisc.edu/wisconsinpress/

3 Henrietta Street
London WC2E 8LU, England

Copyright © 2007
The Board of Regents of the University of Wisconsin System
All rights reserved

1   3   5   4   2

Printed in the United States of America

Library of Congress Cataloging-in-Publication Data
Benderson, Bruce.
Sex and isolation: and other essays / Bruce Benderson.
    p.   cm.
ISBN 0-299-22310-8 (cloth: alk. paper)
ISBN 0-299-22314-0 (pbk.: alk. paper)
    1. Benderson, Bruce—Anecdotes.
    2. Gay men—Sexual behavior—Anecdotes.
    3. Gay culture—United States—Anecdotes.
4. Alienation (Social psychology)—United States—Anecdotes.
    I. Title.
    HQ76.2.U5B46   2007
    306.76'62—dc22   2007011727

Contents

Foreword

CATHERINE TEXIER

What I remember best about my first meeting with Bruce Benderson is the shoes he was wearing that day. My ex-husband, Joel Rose, and I had gone to his apartment on Saint-Mark's Place in the East Village, before he became our neighbor on East 7th Street, to discuss his first contribution to our literary magazine *Between C and D*. The piece Bruce had submitted to us for publication seamlessly wove his sexual encounter with a violent Times Square ex-con hustler with the author's guilty feelings about a visit to New York from his mother. The piece would later be included in *Pretending to Say No,* a collection of short stories. The startling contrasts between the author's raunchy sex life with hardcore criminals and his dutiful feelings toward his beloved mother would become the two poles of Bruce Benderson's work, from his first novel, *User,* to his powerful memoir *The Romanian.*

But back to the shoes. They were pointy buckled creepers, with a vamp made of black-and-white leopard skin, of the kind worn by rockabilly bands along with stovepipe jeans in the fifties, and later favored by punk-rock bands. They were super-trendy — this being the mid-eighties — and impressed me greatly. With his Teddy Boy shoes and his violent sexual history, Bruce was the epitome of cool, dangerous gayhood.

That was more than twenty years ago, but by his writing (not only his shoes), Bruce is still the epitome of cool, dangerous gayhood. Certainly these essays, which cover about a decade, demonstrate again and again how his life of promiscuity and danger has shaped his understanding of the world, and how his unique vantage point illuminates dark corners of the American and Anglo-Saxon psyche with startling insight.

Appearing for the first time in the United States, this collection includes two long pieces, "Sex and Isolation" and "Toward the New Degeneracy," the latter previously published here as a stand-alone book in 1997. A number of the shorter essays are lively reportages and portraits written as magazine assignments, like "Tel Quel's Gaudy Harlequin," a profile of the Paris-based, Cuban writer Severo Sarduy; "Montmartre's Blue Angel," a sketch of the "French Liberace"; and "The Not-So-Secret Life of Consuela Cosmetic," an account of a fearsome transsexual dying of AIDS. My favorite among the portraits is "The Spider Woman's Mother," a hilarious vignette of Argentine writer Manuel Puig (whose novel *The Kiss of the Spider Woman* was made into an Academy Award–winning movie in 1985, and later adapted as a musical on Broadway). Puig, the archetypical "queen," was in the habit of feminizing everyone and everything to the point of total absurdity. Benderson, who had become a close friend, brings his quirky persona to life with wonderful candor and warmth.

But Benderson's two major essays, "Toward the New Degeneracy" and "Sex and Isolation," which articulate with limpid prose the ideas that run through his books and reveal his personal itinerary, are really the centerpieces of this collection. It shouldn't be a surprise to any reader familiar with his work that Bruce's great love affair is his lasting romance with Times Square and its denizens. Anyone who has read his extraordinary novel *User,* an attempt to capture the cosmology that has fascinated him so much—the community of street people, transsexuals, bohemian junkies, dangerous thugs, and hypermasculine Latino hustlers, who populated Times Square before Mayor Giuliani cleaned it up and turned it into a theme park for tourists—will recognize his fictional underworld.

"Toward the New Degeneracy" is a poignant manifesto in favor of the old city nexus, the "downtown," which has its origins in the traditional marketplace, where all social classes rub elbows and mix, economically and sexually. Refusing to play the part of the outsider looking in, Benderson claims the mantle of Norman Mailer's "White Negro," who draws his fierce, sexual energy from the underground classes. For Benderson, being a gay hipster navigating the tough underworld is not a posture; it has been his life. After his foray into the bathhouses of San Francisco in the seventies, accumulating, to his own admission, thousands of sexual encounters, he was hit with terror and the fear of punishment when the AIDS epidemic exploded in the eighties. The period also coincided with his own midlife crisis. After the furious sexual experimentation of his twenties, he was feeling a certain kind of emptiness and loss of identity. He credits *Saul's Book,* by Paul T. Rogers, with turning his fear of dying into a renewed lust for life. The novel, which came out in 1985, was the creation of a social worker and ex-con who was later murdered by the Times Square hustler whom he had adopted. "In Sinbad," Benderson writes about the fictional character of the hustler, "I sensed a much more vital and courageous version of my own despair about AIDS and lost identity. . . . In the age of AIDS I went on a voyage to find the world of Sinbad, hoping to recover that sense of the old 'degeneration' that had once linked underclass energies with the underground avant-garde."

"Toward the New Degeneracy" is the intellectual chronicle of that voyage. "I met people who were much more in danger than me," Bruce told me, "yet were festive about it. It was exciting to have sex and find love with macho, real men, not middle-class homosexual men. It was an opportunity to intimately know another class." What is startling in "Toward the New Degeneracy" is Benderson's passionate defense of the fluidity of gender and class against the "reductive tendencies of class-prejudiced identity politics, with its formula of actions equaling identity" favored by the Anglo-Saxon world. Benderson romanticizes the polymorphous sexuality of the street macho, whom he sees as "homophobic and intensely homosexual at the same time. . . . It's the role he plays that matters, regardless of which sex he does it with. . . . In the culture of poverty . . . the bravado of appearances is one thing, and off-the records experiences and feelings are another. A man's got to have an image but he must not become a slave to it." Benderson rejects rigid gender boundaries just as he rejects rigid sexual boundaries, going as far as arguing for the freedom imparted by the old homosexual "closet," which allows married men, for instance, to experience isolated erotic episodes, and still be intensely attracted to women. "There are sexual impulses that are too fragmented to base an entire sociological identity upon. To brand them simply as 'closeted' is intolerant and presumptuous."

The character of the macho, straight hustler who turns tricks with gay men for money, which appears in *The Roma-nian*, Benderson's memoir of falling obsessively in love with a Romanian hustler, perfectly illustrates that point. For Bruce, getting involved with Romulus, whom he met in Budapest during an assignment for nerve.com, was an attempt to relive the drama of the old Times Square.

"Sex and Isolation," the opening essay of this collection, written a couple of years after "Toward the New Degeneracy" but only published in French so far, opens with an unforgettable scene of Benderson, now confined to his computer, video conferencing a mutual masturbation with a young Egyptian with the tag name "YOUNG WANT OLD," who is wearing only a loincloth, which he will gradually unwrap all the way to reveal his genitals. The scene is both hilarious and profoundly disturbing, as we realize that Benderson, "in place of countless hunts in the streets of mid-town New York for sex, ha[s] succumbed to these continuous electronic swaddlings" because he has no other place to go. The author poignantly laments the disappearance of human encounters, those informal, unofficial "tête-à-têtes" that occurred spontaneously—in the street, in the office, or at school; between the milkman and the housewife, the teacher and the student, the single man and the waitress; some libidinous, some innocent, some in-between—that were neither "mediated" nor "reported."

Again, as he does in "Toward the New Degeneracy," Benderson targets the WASP ethic, along with the disappearance of public spaces and the rise of the Internet, with the increasing monitoring and policing of American life. He argues that the Anglo-Saxon obsession with disclosure—handed down from earlier schools of Protestantism—forms the basis of the American sensibility, making the so-called Paradise promised by America impossible to achieve. He maintains that this obsession with disclosure should be distinguished from the Catholic notion of confession. Born and raised French Catholic, I was particularly intrigued by his distinction. For Benderson, Protestant American disclosure is tantamount to a direct and rigid revelation of truth to God. It is the opposite of what he holds dear: secrets, ambiguity, fluidity, undisclosed encounters, which are much more compatible with the "Latinate emphasis on rhetorical devices that screen and artfully interpret a concealed interior life." Still, even in the heart of a Protestant culture and alone in front of his computer monitor, Benderson manages to play with his persona, using soft or harsh lighting and strategically placed bulbs to create a sweeter or more dominant type in order to seduce his cyber partners.

But that's a poor simulacrum for the real life he has led in the past. In spite of his adaptation to the Internet way of life, Benderson has a quarrel with modernity. He is an old-fashioned libertarian, an anarchist, an advocate for "chaos." He has been compared to Hubert Selby Jr. and Jean Genet, but the comparison is flawed, since they came from the underclass. In his approach he is closer to the Baudelarian character Le Flâneur. He is a true heir of D.H. Lawrence, Henry Miller, and Paul Bowles, the bohemian bourgeois fascinated by the vitality and exoticism of the underclass, and desperately wanting to experience its humanity.

Of course it's a conundrum almost impossible to resolve. How is it possible, after all, for a middle-class American to truly imagine the destitute's point of view? William T. Vollman is another contemporary writer who tries to give voice to the underclass. But he seems to do it gingerly, and in spite of his involvement with prostitutes and the poorest of the poor, he keeps his outsider's stance. Bruce Benderson fearlessly plunges in, dissecting his own passion as deeply as he can, and always showing fairness and compassion.

These essays are a passionate plea for openness instead of segregation, for amorality and compassion instead of judgment and fear, for the noir perversity of the human psyche. They deserve to take their place alongside Norman Mailer's "The White Negro" and Georges Bataille's anti-surrealist *Documents* "against received ideas."

Acknowledgments

The list of people entangled with these essays is several volumes long. Let me, however, highlight several who helped make them possible: Manuel Puig, one of the only true geniuses I have ever known; Richard Milazzo, who first published *Toward the New Degeneracy;* Agnès Guéry-Plazy, my tireless publicist at Editions Payot & Rivages in Paris; my French editors Lidia Breda, François Guérif, and Catherine Argand, who sometimes thought of publishing me before Americans did; Camille Paglia, who urged me to write nonfiction; the legion of homeboys who became my friends and confidantes during the Times Square years and taught me about their world; and Glenn Belverio, for suggesting this title. Thanks also to Raphael Kadushin, Sheila Moermond, and other folks at the University of Wisconsin Press.

Different, shorter, or identical versions of the following essays appeared in these publications and are used by permission (note: all French publications cited were translated from the English by Thierry Marignac):

"Sex and Isolation" in French as *Sexe et solitude* (Paris: Editions Payot & Rivages, 1999, 2001).

"Surrendering to the Spectacle" as "Surrender to the Spectacle: The Value of Entertainment," in *Parallax* 11, no. 2 (April–June 2005): 36–43; in French as "Abandonnez-vous au spectacle," in *Au-delà du spectacle* (November 1999–February 2000), and in Bruce Benderson, *Attitudes* (Paris: Bibliothèque Rivages, 2006), 35–53.

"Fear of Fashion" in the column "New York Lowdown," *Purple* 8 (Summer 2001); in French as "Avoir peur de la mode," in *Beaux Arts* (November 19, 2004), and in *Attitudes,* 54–61.

"America's New Networkers" as "Creative Publicity," in *Vice* 9, no. 5 (December 2002); in French as "Les nouveaux intrigants d'Amerique," in *Attitudes,* 171–83.

"Tel Quel's Gaudy Harlequin" as "All the World's a Drag," in *Lambda Book Report* 4, no. 11 (July–August 1995), copyright © Lambda Rising, Inc., all rights reserved, reproduced by permission of the author; in *Twentieth-Century Literary Criticism,* vol. 167, ed. Thomas J. Schoenberg and Lawrence J. Trudeau (Farmington Hills, Mich.: Thomson Gale, 2005); in French as "L'arlequin criard de Tel Quel," in *Attitudes,* 205–6.

"The Spider Woman's Mother" in French as "La mère de la Femme-Araignée," in *Attitudes,* 135–47.

"Montmartre's Blue Angel" as "Stalking Montmartre's Blue Angel," in *nest* 6 (Fall 1999); in French as "L'Ange bleu de Montmartre," in *Attitudes,* 83–90.

"A Champion in Times Square" in *The Village Voice,* July 2–8, 1997; in French as "Un champion à Times Square," in *Attitudes,* 148–56.

"The Not-So-Secret Life of Consuela Cosmetic" in *New York Press* 11, no. 22 (March 6, 1998); in French as "La vie pas si cachée de Consuela Cosmetic," in *Attitudes,* 157–68.

"Toward the New Degeneracy" as *Toward the New Degeneracy: An Essay* (New York: Edgewise, 1997, 1999); excerpted previously in the print and Internet magazines *Cups, Artnet, Alt-X,* and *Dent;* in French as *Pour un nouvel art dégénéré* (Paris: Editions Payot & Rivages, 1998).

Acknowledgments

I

Mode de Vie

Sex and Isolation

*A*vis: *This is about promiscuity and isolation. The street giving way to the Internet. The end of body contact among the generations. The death of the city as we know it. It is the triumph of the archetypal Protestant—at home and alone with his God.*

Public Space, Virtual Space

I

At first, just swaths of white Egyptian cotton. Then, jerkily, the view tilts up. We both are fraught, I know, with an urge to click the window shut.

Originally published as *Sexe et solitude* (Paris: Editions Payot & Rivages, 1999, 2001).

But we stay on. Nervously, I steal a glance at myself in the color image from my own camera, adjusting it quickly to frame my face and torso.

The other person has leaned back: I can see a slim Egyptian in his twenties, wrapped only in a loincloth. That was the crepelike white cotton that filled the entire screen just a moment ago. Under the image is his handle: YOUNG WANT OLD.

YOUNG WANT OLD and I are about to begin a videoconference by webcam. Perversely attracted by my much older age and greater numbers of both years and pounds, he has decided to take the chance. The pop-up window on my screen asks, <<Do you accept?>>

I click <<yes.>>

Small, cheap, and harmless-looking, my swiveling webcam is attached to the top of my computer screen, which has millions of colors and very high resolution. Fairly simple software is piping me YOUNG WANT OLD's Chaplinesque movements all the way from Egypt. Now he sheds the loincloth. It is a striptease becoming more and more puppetlike—not only because of the paltry frames-per-second of video transmission, but because his eyes are locked on his computer screen, taking in the transmitted image of me.

<<YOUH LUK . . . GOOHD>>, types YOUNG WANT OLD in an Arabic-English full of fantastic misspellings. <<Please movf camera low-her.>> He has unwrapped his loincloth all the way. It coils across one knee like an albino cobra. Then it begins to flap more and more insistently.

YOUNG WANT OLD is masturbating.

<<Move yours lower, too . . .>>, I quickly peck out on the keyboard with my free hand, after which both of us bend forward to adjust our cameras, until our nude bodies become headless torsos pasted side by side on my screen.

<<You veree hairee>>, types YOUNG WANT OLD, as my bandwidth is devoured. Of the two images on my screen, his, coming all the way from Egypt—rather than in a feedback loop like mine—has slowed to a near standstill. YOUNG WANT OLD's movements seem to be taking place in a medium of gelatin. His body and the air around him are broken into sloppy, viscous segments—like two kinds of ectoplasm.

Behind this sluggish layer are other windows, including an Internet chat in a virtual room dubbed New-York-City-Men-4-Men (M4MNYC). I've kept it running during our video—just to up my excitement level. On and on it unfurls, like an inane schizo-conversation, among twenty-three different people who whimsically come and go (<<pics to trade? tops out there?>>). Their babblings are punctuated by primitive pictoforms, clichéd Internet signs meant to substitute for a lack of patience or expressive writing skills: :) = smiling, :(= unhappy or disapproving, :o = oral sex.

Behind the images of YOUNG WANT OLD and myself masturbating, the M4MNYC chat forms a wallpaper of wriggling, spermlike graffiti. These are the virtual bedsheets upon which YOUNG WANT OLD and I now loll. Over all of this is a third window I've got running: the window in which I'm writing this . . .

2

Around the corner of the room in which YOUNG WANT OLD and I are conferencing comes the sound from a television left playing in the background. It punctuates my waking hours with the global noise called "life in America." Certainly *my* life in America has radically changed. In place of countless hunts in the streets of midtown New York for sex, I've succumbed to these continuous electronic swaddlings. Naked but cocooned, I stay home, virtually caressing a supposed world in images like that of YOUNG WANT OLD.

Why have I fallen and turned from a courageous voyageur into an armchair voyeur? The answer to that is simple. *I have nowhere to go.* From the television swarm wishes, threats, jokes, and recriminations—all claiming to be from *somewhere else.* Desire scrawls its inane meanderings on the cathode-ray screen. Buzzing from the tube and squiggles on my computer screen are my new landscape. These energies seem senselessly and fanatically ordered, as in a hive of bees. Their information networks emotionlessly enlace me in vapid caresses. Not since the invention of the printing press has so much disembodied human consciousness been spread so thin. My countrymen have reached the dreary end of exhibitionism, with its aggressions and its passivities, and all that I can do is offer my little part to the spectacle. My hand rises from my groin, to show to the Web camera filaments of semen caught between my fingers and becoming part of this evidence, just before YOUNG WANT OLD and I ruthlessly disconnect.

3

We are very much alone. Nothing leaves a mark. Today's texts and images may look like real carvings—or like specks and stains on a white sheet—but in the end they are erasable, only a temporary blockage of all-invasive light. No matter how long the words and pictures stay on our screens, there will be no encrustation; all will be reversible. Being squirms across the glowing white page of the computer screen, and on closer inspection it becomes cathode patterns flickering and waving on a temporary ground.

4

The global information world is the polar opposite of the physical space called the marketplace, or downtown, which I memorialized in my recent writings. Smell and touch have been exiled from it. Nothing sinks in or keeps its shape. Nothing is remembered in the flesh, which means, quintessentially, the end of long-term memory.

Caressing motions, different kinds of coaxing, promises signed only with screen names, images of open mouths . . . all disappear.

No reply, suddenly. The closing of the center city is loneliness for everyone. The abandonment of the body is isolation, the triumph of pure fantasy.

A writer's dream? Hardly. The stone/flint discordance of interclass tension that happened on the street has stopped producing sparks and, as a consequence, anecdotes.

This is the moment when the ethic of *suburb-inanity* triumphs. Isolated units of identical cubicles. Provincial

America as global conqueror. Could there be a more grotesque, less Modernist, proposal? In 1946 the utopian American suburbs began inventing the isolation to which the age of information appeals. It recast the Victorian drawing room as an electronic holding cell. Now I'm locked inside.

5

Space before cyberspace. On the road. In 1965, still a teenager, and inspired by *City of Night* and *On the Road,* I left my suburban home in Syracuse, New York, and began hitchhiking across country with my boyhood crush Jeffrey. Just a small knapsack of clothing and a sleeping bag. Two hundred dollars to share. Wearing jeans, work shirts and Wellington boots, we stood for four hours at the entrance to a thruway in Buffalo, the cars whizzing by.

It was hot and dusty. Near the end of the afternoon, a vinyl-roofed car with whitewall tires screeched across the blacktop to a dead stop. A man in shirtsleeves leaned through the open window and barked for us to get inside. I climbed into the front seat, my friend in back. The man gave us one glance only. "You must be hustlers," he sneered. Thrilled by the coincidental reference to *City of Night,* I eagerly agreed. We rushed on in silence thirty to forty miles above the speed limit.

Later, the shriek of sirens. The state trooper pulls over our driver. My friend and I sit hunched in our seats, as a black-booted cop crunches gravel in the direction of the car. He won't pull him in this time, however. It turns out our driver's brother is a state trooper, too.

We inch toward the next exit. "Open the glove compartment," hisses the driver. When I do, I find a gun inside.

"Hand it to me."

Mute and dazed, I obey. The handle feels dry, ordinary. But he had asked for the gun only because he feared a search at the toll booth. With ostentatious cool, he twirls the weapon on a finger, before stashing it under his seat.

We climbed out of the car at the exit. We slept beneath an underpass that night.

6

From 1964 until the end of the Vietnam War in 1975, the wide open spaces of our country were colonized by children like us, fleeing the limitations of suburban space. We came from anodyne social environments and were absolutely nonchalant about car travel. From every suburb or small city, we set out on foot with outstretched thumbs, in cars, on motorcycles, or in Volkswagen buses all across the country—as if there were nothing or no one in it that had not been created for our fulfillment. Our adolescent army spread west—not just to San Francisco but also to communes in the Russian River area of California, to New Mexico, Oregon, and Washington State. Perhaps not since the Crusades had such an idealistic but naively xenophobic migration like ours swallowed up public space. Our optimism was the polar opposite of the cynical nativism of the big-city American teenager, typified then and now by the race- and class-conscious New Yorker brought up in urban congestion, whose familiarity with every ethnicity makes him ready with a judgment. We were, instead, impulsive yet protected children, myopic about class differences, open to all but offensively naive. Our Children's Crusade bore as its standard a sense of entitlement about the luxury of mobility. In a few cases, our faddish invasions actually led to the cultural takeover of entire towns by our neo-Buddhist or Hindu cults and communes. Today's Maharishi University of Management, founded by the advocates of Transcendental Meditation, comprises a large part of the population of Fairfield, Iowa; and the followers of Indian guru Bhagwan Shree Rajneesh once seized control of the government of Antelope, Oregon, temporarily changing its name to City of Rajneesh.

In many cases, as we grew older we were slowly absorbed back into bourgeois-controlled space—on an economic level below that to which our hard-working parents had struggled to bring us. Although we may have been easy riders eager for thrills, there was still something deeply Protestant about our antimaterialism. We had a missionary mentality that associated the rejection of style and luxury with Waldenian fantasies of purity and authenticity.

I was one of these pilgrims seeking the kingdom of Pleasure. The guiding factor in my adolescent journey was the need to find an adult with whom to act out a sexual awakening. Without ever planning to encounter the streets of New York, I fantasized about the feel of the sexual underworld—as described in the Beat novel *City of Night*. How can I explain the adolescent experience of reading a book about the surly world of male prostitution, fascinated by the cold despair of the characters, yet strangely unaware that such experiences had to have taken place in the context of the super-city?

There were, however, stories circulating that managed to penetrate the amusement-park trance my fellow suburbanites and I had fabricated. During my trip across country, a college-aged hitchhiker outside of Amarillo, Texas, told me one. He and his girlfriend had been thumbing their way through the southwestern desert. An aging sheriff near a tiny town abducted them at gunpoint and drove them to his ranch in the remote hills, where they were locked in separate cages for two and a half days, brought out only at several intervals to undergo bouts of forced sex together while he watched. The scenario had the flavor of interclass and intergenerational tension. The object of his anger was what he assumed was their lifestyle, loose sexuality and carefree mobility, middle-class privileges that he had been denied.

7

My adolescent journey west brought me to a floor in the Berkeley apartment of several people my age, whose hookah-owning neighbors treated me to daily sessions of marijuana and hashish. A few days later, I went across the bay to San Francisco in search of my whoring experience. I don't remember how I discovered where the young male prostitutes hung out, but I ended up on a street in the Tenderloin, a smaller version of New York's Times Square, where the lowest echelon of street hustling took place. I was still underage, so the only club I could enter had no alcohol. Despite this G-rated feature, the walls reverberated with attitude. Lit only by black light, the hard-edged players were mostly black cross-dressers from the ghetto, sporting acidic oranges and reds or fluorescent white. The experience became a glorious urban shock treatment. My senses overloaded with the compressed atmosphere of rage and sexuality, but I stood unmoving near the bar, a wallflower. The shock of plunging head and shoulders into the city as night was overpowering. How could I ever resist it again?

I hit the sidewalk. A drunken businessman was stumbling out of a nearby bar. With my eyes blanked and feet planted, I thrust my pelvis insolently forward. He gestured me to follow but could barely keep his balance. At Market Street, he began hailing drunkenly for a cab, but each warily passed us by.

As I watched him fumbling with loose bills that were about to spill out of his jacket pocket, I resolved to carry through the project. The idea of a father figure in a pipe-rack suit, passing out in a blandly middle-class hotel room, after which I would go through his pockets and split, was a promise of cocky mastery in my reckless mind. But the man had become frustrated at having to wait for a cab, and he began teetering down the street. I didn't follow him.

Just a short time later, a gleaming black Mercedes with tinted windows pulled up, and the driver leaned out to ask if I wanted to climb inside. I did. He was a stocky man of about forty with a pockmarked face who said he was a choreographer in Las Vegas. I was tongue-tied and falsely sullen, like a fresh violet. I let him drive up a steep series of hills higher and higher into a black night. The altitude produced a stronger and stronger sense of isolation. We parked at Coit Tower, with a view of the city. I waited impatiently for the moment that his hand would touch my leg. When it finally did, I blurted out my artless declaration: sorry, but I would have to ask for money because I hadn't eaten.

Not just awkward, fairly unpleasant sex with a much older body, but fifteen dollars later pressed into my palm was what parted a curtain to reveal an entirely new segment of my life. Urban contamination anointed my adulthood, and from that moment on I wore my impurity like a badge.

To get back from California, Jeffrey and I hitchhiked to Sacramento and found the freight yard. Some railroad bums pointed out an open boxcar but cautioned us to keep it jammed open with a piece of wood. If the door happened to slam shut while the train was moving, we'd be locked in until someone decided to check. Skeletons had been found as the result of such a mishap, for sometimes freight cars weren't opened for weeks at a time.

Unaware of the route we were taking, we eventually found ourselves high in the Sierra Nevada mountains. We had hopped the train with only light jackets and without food or water, thinking there would be frequent stops along the way. Instead, the journey continued for more than twenty-four hours. As we climbed higher and higher into the mountains, the temperature dropped lower and lower. We spent the night with chattering teeth, clutched in each other's arms. Mid-morning of the next day, covered with grime, we saw from the open door of our freight car that we were traveling through desert. We hung our feet out of the train to warm them in the sun and decided to avail ourselves of our only resource, the single joint one of us had saved. As soon as we had smoked it, we thought we had begun to hallucinate. Puddles began to appear in the desert sand. They grew larger: pools of liquid turquoise in a moon landscape of white salt. Finally, they connected with each other into a vast body of water. It wasn't until later that we realized we were looking at Utah's Great Salt Lake.

A few years later, at the age of twenty-two, I found my way back to San Francisco; although my existence there became that of a middle-class drop-out, centering on public assistance, health foods, and promiscuity, from time to time I gravitated back toward the sleazy Tenderloin, where I had had my first experience as a sex worker. Then, during one period of despair, I left my apartment for several months and lived in the streets of the Tenderloin under a made-up name.

8

To ensure the protection of the nuclear family and cope with the problem of increased crime rates in the city, our suburbs tried to excise from adolescence the kinds of experience just described. They were health risks for middle-class children, but they also complicated exclusionary policies concerning class, age, and race because of the unpredictable encounters they fostered.

In small cities like Syracuse, in which I grew up before the time of malls, opportunities for such contact were still possible before the 1970s. My father worked downtown in a neo-gothic turn-of-the-century office building. My visits to it were brief, but I remembered them with longing. It was a world where people existed magically unaccompanied by family members. These shopkeepers, lawyers, cleaning ladies, unmarried secretaries, cigarette-smoking drop-outs, truants, cripples, window washers, bachelor hairdressers, dentists, elevator operators, chiropractors, accountants, soda jerks, bellboys, cleaning ladies, construction workers, vagrants, alcoholics, divorced barmaids, and probation officers ate in public places rather than at home. Astonishingly, they lived lives separate from the family circle.

Who under thirty and living in a small or medium-sized American city can remember the old-fashioned department store smelling of furniture polish with great rooms full of merchandise, like some catalogued inventory for fetishists, or its block-long series of windows with surreal landscapes involving mannequins? Its uniformed elevator operators, highly made-up perfume clerks, gloves on plaster manikin hands, lingerie cases, torsos in girdles, and largely unmonitored dressing rooms (yes, a clerk touched me in one of them, when I was about eleven) promised vague, unhealthy pleasures.

I remember our town's several great department stores because they were the central loci of my fantasy world from the time I first visited one, at four and a half years old, holding my mother's hand, to buy an Eaton suit with a matching woolen cap. Aside from the mirrors and odors, there was the strange, light touch of the tape-measure-wielding tailor and the presence of my mother in her stiff, gray suit standing nearby.

9

Today practical activities (work, shopping) are regimented. Shopping has lost its eroticism of extending throughout a *terrain.* Grim supply depots called malls and outlets have taken the place of the old fantasy landscapes. Military in their uniformity, anonymous, and shorn of either their high-bourgeois sophistication or their mom-and-pop familiarity, shopping sites now have a cookie-cutter, insipid brightness. Transportation to and from these stations is confined to individual family vehicles; travel by foot is left to the few who are both underage and unsupervised, or to the destitute; public transportation is only for the handicapped or elderly.

My father's office building—with its polished terrazzo floors, candy-and-cigarette counter in the lobby, orange-lit marble hallways—has been supplanted by a suburban office complex with an anonymous carport. Destinations have been denatured. *They no longer represent any radical departure from home.* No longer are errands interwoven with the erotic landscape of the street.

10

Pre-seventies American life was the era of the unofficial tête-à-tête: the tryst between the milkman and the housewife, the businessman and his secretary who worked late, adolescents in the locker rooms after the game, coaches living with their mothers and supplying certain boys with money for catcher's mitts and candy, teachers giving students after-school homework help, the single man living in the downtown hotel and the greasy-spoon waitress, the traveling salesman and the manicurist on a lunch break. Unlike the information age in which I now live, these worlds were not mediated by the supreme value of *disclosure.* And that value—disclosure—represents the real triumph of the

Protestant ethic. It is, however, a peculiar kind of disclosure without *commitment* or *utility*, a phenomenon I will discuss further on.

But at the time, many libidinal experiences were unreported. On the surface of the small urban community were convention, discipline, and prejudice. But partly because spatial structures allowed so many chances for actual contact (the bus station, the dining car of the train, the playing field, the main library, the museum, the gym, the hotel lobby, the fitting room, the lavatory, and the downtown street corner), my life in pre-seventies America was secretly eccentric; it had multiple dark corners for misbehavior. It had a bus station where adolescents could experiment with cruising adults. It had large, old-fashioned libraries with unmonitored corners.

II

One type of secret pre-information-age interaction involved intergenerational liaisons with adolescents. Teachers and students, transients and experimenting teenage boys: all found niches in this older structure. I'm talking about a phenomenon that served as a primary tool of sex education for adolescents before sex education was considered an intellectually imparted knowledge and was taken over by community groups, psychologists, and the public school system.

Imagine, then, my astonishment when I saw the pinched face of the suburban fifteen-year-old on *Court TV*, accusing his high school teacher, a woman in her early thirties, of having sex with him. The teacher was caught by the camera sobbing and denying the charge of statutory rape. This is the label for any sex act, no matter how consenting, between a

Sex and Isolation

17

person over eighteen and a person under. Accordingly, no matter how willing the hormone-riddled fifteen-year-old may have been, he had now become the victim of this woman.

I thought about the locker-room talk from my own teenage years and tried to edit it to fit the current story. Back then, boys who were fifteen or sixteen would have crowed about the conquest of an older woman. And if she were the teacher, that was an extra feather in their cap. What better way to assert manhood and strengthen the male ego than taking Teach' herself for a tumble? In a parallel manner, my early experience as a male prostitute is more important to me than many of my other adolescent accomplishments. It represents both mastery over an older person, rebellion from an overprotective home, and a lawless moment of secret, unacknowledged nurturing from a father figure.

12

This reversal of machismo, in which the already physically mature male can be imagined as sexual victim, is not a symptom of fallout from feminism. It is, rather, a logical outcome of recent cultural and legal changes affecting the status of the young. It also has to do with the death of public space and the confinement of children within the family circle. This becomes most obvious when one examines specific laws pertaining to childhood. Traditionally, children outside the context of their families have been earmarked by the state for protection and confinement. Eventually, the two categories of protection and confinement got lumped together, and the state has come to see no breach of individual rights in the widespread latitude of determination about what protects a child. In 1980 a liberal law allowing adolescents the option of leaving their homes and seeking shelter through other private or public sources was made much narrower by allowing children to run away from home only once without detention. Then, during the 1980s, the mood of Congress moved more and more drastically in the direction of child containment, with a special emphasis on preventing children from running away to big cities. The official rule of thumb, as set forth by the Reagan administration, became: "Children have a right to family, not to independence."

13

One of the most grotesque and ironic documents about the hypocrisies of child protection written at that time was by Father Bruce Ritter, a supporter of the Reagan administration, which financed his network of urban youth shelters as a way of showing that the answer to aid to dependent children lay in private charity rather than in the welfare system. Ritter's book *Sometimes God Has a Kid's Face* was distributed in 1988 as a public-relations tool and featured his Times Square shelter for adolescents, Covenant House. The book combined detailed descriptions of the lifestyles of runaway adolescent prostitutes of both sexes with religious homilies about child protection. At one point Ritter describes hugging an adolescent male stripper in Times Square as a way of showing him that love doesn't necessarily come in an exploitation package.

I would see Ritter occasionally in the streets of Times Square, frozen-eyed and smiling grimly, his neck stiff in a clerical collar. The fact that no donor seemed to notice the prurient fascination lurking beneath the piety in Ritter's books suggests a willful ignorance of subtext. When several adolescent boys later accused Ritter of pressuring them into sexual liaisons, *Sometimes God Has a Kid's Face* became pornography. Ritter was asked to step down from his post.

14

Ritter never admitted that children's sexual power provides a major covert mandate for their control and protection. One could say that family bonding partly depends upon the tension between incestuous urges and their prohibition. These urges are sublimated into various forms of discipline, nurturing, physical contact, or accusation. The hot hide-and-seek of family desire, transference, and denial has been termed *family romance* by psychoanalysts. Its energies provide one part of the magnetism of the domestic nest. That nest becomes most claustrophobic when it is cordoned off from other social realities, which is exactly what happened in the suburban community. Whereas the necessities of city life invented the independent child, the suburbs *reversed* this phenomenon and reinvented the late adolescent—and even post-adolescent—as a dependent.

15

In provincial America, the wholesale definition of late-adolescent individuals as non-autonomous minors sometimes represses perverse urges to fantasize about children as the opposite, to imagine them as strangely lurid simulacra of adults. These urges come up in more and more grotesque form in isolated areas where the only reality is the circle of the family. One of the most curious manifestations of this phenomenon seems to be the child beauty pageant. These competitions involve dressing little girls as miniature, mincing adults, complete with extravagant hairstyles, full makeup, high heels, and fetching glances. It is true that the world's museums are full of portraits from other centuries of children in adult dress because the modern concept of childhood was only recently invented. But in the current climate of worry about child predators, when it comes to images of children in adult dress, the girls appear infinitely more tarted up than in the past, and they are more pornographic than pictures of, say, totally naked children frolicking on the beach, some of which have recently been seized even from their parents as examples of prurient photography.

The most bizarre celebrity to come from the child pageant culture is, of course, JonBenet Ramsey, the six-year-old Boulder, Colorado, beauty queen who was discovered murdered more than a decade ago. The unsolved crime hangs like a puzzling cloud over America, symbolic of its ambivalence about the objectification of childhood, its confusion between parental protection and parental exploitation; no one can escape its troubling images, since literally hundreds of pictures of Ramsey in furs, feather boas, tiaras, or miniskirts have been distributed by the media. No matter how many pictures of the deceased six-year-old one sees, they never lose their shockingly prurient ambiguity; but we are apparently so in need of socially acceptable outlets for these impulses that we never say the photos provide such a thrill.

Such sudden, shocking and unavowed eruptions of bad taste are, I believe, pure products of the provincial Protestant American imagination. Within the peculiar structuring of libido characteristic of this imagination, which began in colonial America but has been adapted to the sprawling suburbs, exceptional wishes and impulses have no choice but to pop up in strangely fragmented and irresponsible fashion—in defiance of pious equations of social hygiene. However, unsettling pictures of little girls dressed as fetching adults are hardly the least astonishing examples. In 1988, in Olympia, Washington, a city with more than its fair share of both fundamentalist and New Age religious cults, occurred an explosion of accusations and mea culpa that were as astounding as some of the recorded testimonies of the Puritans' Salem witch trials.

Paul R. Ingram, a deputy of the sheriff's department and chairman of the local Republican Party who was a strict Pentecostal, was accused by his adult daughter of past long-term sexual abuse. She had had what was termed a "recovered memory" of these incidences during a retreat directed by a charismatic Christian leader, and now she came forward with shocking allegations. It should be kept in mind that, at least on the surface, Ingram's daughter and her siblings had been brought up by her father and mother, who ran a day-care center at home, under the most puritanical conditions. As Pentecostals, they believed that sex was not a topic to be discussed with children and that popular libidinal outlets for youth, such as sports and rock music, were inevitably

Mode de Vie

unhealthy. The Ingrams lived a storybook rural lifestyle, with picturesque elements evoking the individualism and self-sufficiency of the American frontier, including their own farm animals and a vegetable garden. Their entire life was rigidly centered within the confines and values of the nuclear family, which perhaps in part explains why that life was about to be violently sundered.

When confronted with his daughter's "recovered memories" of years of sexual abuse, the deeply pious father stated that he had no memory of having been an abuser; but since he believed his daughter had firm religious convictions, he was willing to try to bring to consciousness these acts through some careful self-searching. What followed is astonishing but not at all limited to a single incident or region in provincial America. In the cell in which he had once locked others, the deputy sheriff spent a lot of time praying, often with his pastor, who encouraged him to make a full *disclosure.*

When Ingram was alone, he sometimes practiced relaxation techniques and would imagine going into a thick fog. In this trance state, what he identified as real memories would suddenly appear before him, and he would write them all down.

In this way father and daughter collaborated from a distance and, between the two of them, produced much more extreme allegations. Their narrative grew into a scenario of satanic abuse involving every member of the family and, eventually, other colleagues at the sheriff's office. All were accused of involving the family in elaborate sexual rituals, ostensibly when the men came to the house for poker parties, starting when the children were very young. The rituals included forced fellatio, anal intercourse, group orgies, urination, the smearing of feces, sex with animals, and even the murder of newborn babies.

Apparently, and at least for a time, each victim and each alleged perpetrator was in agreement that such events had taken place. All seemed to recover these memories bit by bit in trance states that had a disturbingly dissociated, emotionless quality, which the investigators attributed to the deeply traumatic nature of the memories.

By the time of this incident, similar satanic abuse survivor stories in the thousands had begun to flood the offices of therapists, detectives, and journalists, as well as daytime talk shows. The movement centering on the idea of satanic abuse had started in 1980, when a Canadian woman and her therapist wrote a book called *Michelle Remembers,* which describes satanic sexual rituals presumably undergone by the writer at the hands of her parents and other adults. Beginning with the publication of this book, North America marked a time when accusations regarding satanic sexual abuse ripped apart several communities. The accusers were usually adult female children, but sometimes the source of the accusations were toddlers who had been subject to purportedly helpful questioning by social workers and other authorities. In more than one incident, the accusations revolved around alleged activities in day-care centers.

So common did these charges become in the 1980s that satanic-ritual abuse (SRA) became the subject of several medical and psychological papers. Some researchers have connected fantasies about it to dissociative identity disorder, but they have also noted an amazing similarity in reports from widely divergent areas of the country. People spoke of being drugged, being penetrated sexually with various devices, being forced to watch animal sacrifices, being buried alive with the corpses of babies, being smeared with feces, being forced into cannibalism, and taking part in the rituals of Satan while they were hypnotized. Although physical evidence of a network of satanic abusers has never been uncovered, and the recovered memories may be fantasies or suggestions induced during a hypnotic trance, a significant percentage of psychotherapists believe they are true, a position that has bolstered the cultural respectability of SRA and led to its acceptance as a prosecutorial tool in court as well as material for outrage within some sectors of the Christian fundamentalist movement. One of the major features of SRA is supposed to be mind control, which not only forces the victim to comply but also keeps him or her from mentioning these incidences afterward. Other reasons given for lack of hard evidence for satanic abuse are that Satanists eat their victims or dispose of them in secret hiding places or keep their child pornography locked in a network of special vaults around the country.

The SRA survivor movement cannot be definitively distinguished from elements of the incest survivor movement, which was originally generated by left-wing feminism—those activists who were finally speaking out about years of incestuous sexual molestation by fathers, uncles, or older brothers. However, the dividing line between liberal anti-incest activists and conservative child protectionists is a blurry one. Still, the militancy about incest that gained force on the Left, even if it included ideology about recovered memories, was a long way away from a focus on hypnotically induced memory. The latter makes an appeal to Freud's early theory of repressed incest experiences—one he later repudiated by recasting recovered incest memory as fantasy. No one will ever know for sure whether some or all of the satanic abuse accusations are true. But whether or not they are, their construction and polymorphous perversity are an example of the overweening sexual fantasy life of Puritan America. Such a tendency has often manifested itself as reaction formation—in accusation—and only gathers enough charge to erupt in communities that resemble the traditional tightly knit religious communes that produced Salem.

17

Within the new climate of fear about sexual predators, no one seems to remember that intergenerational sex between adolescents over the age of fourteen and adults was once a left-wing linchpin. It was a direct result of the now old-fashioned urban value of contact. One function of "downtown," or the center city, was the space it provided young people for sexual experimentation. And until recently, America had some noteworthy left-wing utopian activists who wanted to lower the age of sexual consent. This was, in fact, advanced as a political ideal by Allen Ginsburg and some of the yippies as well as the founders of the early gay liberation movement. It's hard to believe today that intergenerational sex was once thought of as a healthful political aspiration in the left-wing community; yet even Paul Goodman, psychotherapist, novelist, poet, and teacher, who wrote *Growing Up Absurd,* a radical critique of the institutionalized treatment of youth in America, outspokenly advocated the libidinal mentor-student relationship of the ancient Greeks. At least for some gay men (including myself), adolescent encounters with older men in the big cities are treasured memories of sexual awakening. They appear to us as first experiences with understanding minds outside of the oppressive framework of the nuclear family in our flight from the bland suburban community. In fact, any serious concern about the exploitation of physically mature individuals (ages fifteen to eighteen) by those who are older is a very, very recent phenomenon in this country. Codified outrage concerning it is barely over twenty-five years old.

Today's assimilationist gay liberationists are loathe to admit it, but a benchmark of the gay movement occurred in 1978, when a group of gay men formed the Boston/Boise Committee to combat a conservative district attorney who was exploiting a homosexual case of child molestation as a reelection strategy. Gore Vidal was involved in a fund-raiser for the committee, which eventually sponsored a conference on man-boy love and the age of consent. An Episcopal bishop, some social workers, and a psychiatrist participated in this conference, a caucus of which led to the founding of the North American Man Boy Love Association. At the time, the most salient features of this now maligned organization were neo-Marxist, and at different times its members have protested against corporal punishment, the draft, compulsory schooling, and intervention in El Salvador. NAMBLA members, though some may be naive utopianists, have also endorsed the right of even young children to serve on juries, vote, hold office, and make their own living arrangements.

Though currently the most publicized feature of this organization is its insistence on legalizing intergenerational sex, over the years it has also been concerned with radical children's liberation, and some percentage of the activities of members is devoted to literary and theoretical analyses of American culture's treatment of youth—as in the writings of Paul Goodman.

Until very recently, intergenerational contact was merely a corollary to the sexual liberationist theories of the pioneers of the urban gay movement beginning in the 1960s. Consider, for example, the case of Harry Hay, recently deceased, whose initial political activism began with his membership in the Communist Party. In 1950, he and his lover, Rudi Gernreich (who would later became famous for designing the topless dress and topless bathing suit), launched the precursor to contemporary gay liberation known as the Mattachine Society, named after the satirical French Renaissance folk dance performed by the fraternities of clerics known as the *sociétés joyeuses*. Hay's writings and declarations embody the earliest and, in many ways, the most radical statements about gay identity and eventually came to include the idea that gays and lesbians might be a third gender and a separate people, whose necessary, positive roles in society and even in evolution could be traced back to Neolithic times and some Native American cultures. Hay's positing of a third gender, which only occurred to him later in life, was in part an attack on binary thinking, as typified by the Hegelian foundations of strict Marxist theory, with which he eventually grew disillusioned. He was also one of the first gay liberationists to denounce an earlier gay activist strategy of casting homosexual acts as victimless crimes on a par with drug use and prostitution, because he believed this obscured the positive role of the homosexual in society and history. Like Allen Ginsburg, he was a theoretical supporter of intergenerational sexual contact, because he was painfully aware of the deep need of homosexual youth to seek information about sexual identity and sexual experience outside of the home and established institutions. His vision eventually became New Age and partly Reichian, asserting that the full expression of the human sprit bypasses the repression of sexuality and that sexuality is a prime means of self-discovery and healing.

18

In 1994, ultraconservative senator Jesse Helms pushed through a resolution denying U.S. funding to the United Nations until it could prove that it did not officially support any organization that promoted pedophilia. Helms's measure was aimed specifically at the International Lesbian and Gay Association (ILGA), an umbrella group for thousands of diverse gay organizations, including NAMBLA. Although his strategy centered ostensibly on sexual morality, it was symptomatic of the profound distrust between his provincial constituency in the South, who opposed American involvement in international issues, and the policy-makers and media giants of the cities. In the crisis that ensued, ILGA delegates voted to expel NAMBLA, thus hoping to retain its affiliation with the United Nations, which was now also assured American funding. In the meantime, the controversy produced a schism between the gay movement's two main strands: liberationist and assimilationist. Already in his mid-eighties, Hay gave an impassioned speech to ILGA, imploring them not to divide the gay movement by expelling any group from it, including NAMBLA. Nevertheless, his voice was drowned out by louder factions bent on mainstream acceptance and shocked by what they interpreted as his support of intergenerational pairing.

19

Harry Hay's ideas refer back to a time when people still believed in cosmopolitan values and in history as continuous and connected. His Modernist opinions were developed in the cauldron of contact characteristic of urban life. Hay used history to dignify and legitimize gay identity. The America in which we now live seems to be becoming more and more insular. It is a narcissistic chamber in which the only narratives deemed legitimate are personal or family-oriented, often derived from the therapeutic testimonies of the Protestant-inspired self-help movement and unmediated by the strong sense of diversity that used to come from urban living. This new tendency is, in many ways, reminiscent of early-American Protestant communities with their practice of giving testimony before God and their peers. And such testimonies in the form of talk-show appearances or recovery meetings are now a form of entertainment. They appeal to the journalistic genres of the documentary and the "human interest" story.

At the time of this writing, on the TV around the corner of my L-shaped room, the impeachment of President Clinton is in progress. In fact, it is, astonishingly, the best sex show that the Republicans have ever offered. The droning points of order bark from the cheap television speaker, and dull voices ask their endless questions of endless witnesses. A few days later, Monica Lewinsky appears on television with Barbara Walters to tell us that the President is a "good kisser." Never before has bureaucracy been so *libidinized.*

This scandal, which inspired so much global contempt of America, has, despite the blasé comments of European media and government officials, been completely misunderstood. Never for a moment did it seriously involve issues of sexual morality or represent a truly puritanical reaction to adultery. Response to the uncovering of the Clinton-Lewinsky affair on both the Left and the Right points to a peculiar phenomenon of Americana that no other culture has been able to grasp. This phenomenon, as mentioned earlier, is concerned with the issue of *disclosure* of and for itself. But fully understanding the American need for disclosure requires some familiarity with the earlier schools of Christianity that formed the bases of the American sensibility. Although the disclosure to which I am referring often involves the avowal of one's faults or transgressions, it has little if anything to do with the Catholic notion of confession. It is, instead, a testimony without intermediary between the individual and the element supposed to represent the reality principle. Such an element is bipartite: it is composed of God and the community.

American disclosure is historically typified in this country by the Religious Society of Friends, or Quakers, who believe, like some other Protestant sects, that divine revelation comes in a split second to each individual. A direct relationship to God has a radical effect upon speech. It ensures that simple sincerity, self-monitored each moment for honesty, clarity, and well-meaning, will remain the only means of verbal communication. In fact, the Quakers once believed so strongly in this principle that they refused to engage in bargaining, maintaining that such an activity was impossible because truth was not flexible. In a Quaker religious meeting, any member of the congregation can stand and give verbal testimony; this accords such gatherings great spontaneity and encourages outbursts of plainspoken revelation. Americans consider the Latinate emphasis on rhetorical devices that screen and artfully interpret a concealed interior life or the real facts behind a political controversy neither efficacious, nor discreet, nor representative of any complex relationship to truth. Thus, the entire reaction of this country to the Clinton-Lewinsky affair was based on an anxiety about whether or not Clinton's mouth, eyes, gestures, and words conveyed *absolute honesty.* By *absolute,* I am referring to a nonrelativist concept in which nothing stands between the speaker and his Maker.

20

Unfortunately, the astonishing frankness of American disclosure has of late been bowdlerized by several factors. It has finally become polluted by another distinctly American ethic, and that is the ethic of pragmatism; for, as Max Weber hinted in his 1905 text, *The Protestant Ethic and the Spirit of Capitalism,* the historical development of the Protestant value system may exist in its beginnings as an ascetic philosophy, but is bound to descend into total utilitarianism.

21

As disclosure became hybridized with pragmatism, it degenerated into a pop version of itself, one lacking in commitment. Confessions blurted out at self-help meetings or on daytime talk shows temporarily offer the epiphanic galvinization enjoyed by the early Protestant sects, who believe in lightning-quick insight through salvation; but what is missing from the formula is such a sect's community, which demands commitment and endurance based on such language. Instead, there is an exaggerated demand coming from the market and the global information culture for adaptation to constantly changing conditions. If you think the loss of privacy in America is a question of surveillance and the infringement of rights, you are only partly correct. For many have testified that the most intimate-seeming disclosure (the talk show, the documentary, the televised court trial, the newspaper interview) feels profoundly therapeutic and provides a means to air and review a traumatic incident and experience a feeling of cleansing. However, with the expulsion of these utterances from the lips seems to come a tabula rasa—not just for the speaker but also for the spectator—a mindless new beginning that, in many ways, makes the experience superficial. Without commitment to the future, Protestant disclosure has lost its temporal dimension. Its effects don't last. In politics, of course, disclosure—sincerity, revelation, and commitment—is merely rhetorical style, a realization that upset so many Americans during the Clinton-Lewinsky scandal.

22

Thus, secret spaces, commensurate with urban space and adolescent sexual experiments, are disappearing, to make room for a new, mindless kind of transparency. The age of information is bringing the question of Protestant disclosure and commitment to new levels of degeneration. At the same time, electronic communication is offering maximum disclosure, increased speed of exposure and, conversely, increased anonymity. You can say or show practically anything over electronic media, and then you can make it all disappear with a touch of the delete button. And, of course, there are numerous opportunities for hiding your identity. Your supposedly heartfelt remarks—about politics, sexual fantasies, health, aggression, guilt, or empathy—are subject to no extensive critique or demand for follow-up. In the majority of cases, you are not called upon to stand up for your words or behavior. They become like billboards or fleeting sounds seen and heard from a passing train; or, at their best, brief interludes lived while traveling on vacation, always to be remembered viscerally in a few isolated cases, but absolutely untraceable.

The same is doubly true of the purely sexual encounter on the Internet. Beneath the rich opportunities for role-play, fantasy, and emotional exploration, there is something hardened and cynical about cyber-conjugation. It's as ruthless as certain other forms of promiscuous sex: you're well aware that you're erotically manipulating neuroses, needs, fears, and aggressions, but the possibility of a quick exit provides an amoral kind of boldness. It's a ping-pong competition in which part of the fun and the game is to keep your own vulnerability protected.

23

<<Use me to get off, 31 years. I'm the type who likes to give head and enjoys exciting older guys. I like guys who know what they want and are ready, willing, and able to use me. Real men, ones who know how to take control. Ones who have no qualms about zipping up their fly and walking away just as soon as they get off. I'll please you by mouth at your place or in a hotel. Once a week is great, but use me just once if that's what you like. I'm submissive for the right kind of man. NYCReady>>

<<Hey, Ready, I could use your services. I've been called the bear type: big and stocky and covered with hair. I'm older. I've got your age beat by more than a decade. I know how to take control. Send me a photo, and I'll send you mine. Then maybe we can get together and see what happens. You may find me more than a mouthful.>>

As I've already stated, the majority of attempts to bring cyber fantasy to the "real" world end up scuttled. That is why this encounter ended before it began with the following message:

<<Just idly wondering if you are some kind of perverted bottom who gets off wasting somebody's evening!!! COULDN'T have missed me in that bar, as I was the only guy who looked like I described. Fuck it, it's probably not much of a loss, you're probably a real dog anyway. Have a happily submissive life. You're lousy at it!>>

As the meeting draws near, it points toward a rude encounter with the physical that threatens to exterminate pleasure and supplant it with anxiety. In many ways, an actual meeting points to real, rather than simulated, disclosure. For the same reason, encounters that actually do work seem to happen on a physical level that occurs much more immediately. People who live in the same city and are ready for sex may meet in a chat room and connect right away. Someone types a phone number, and here is a brief conversation. Or, in some cases, the encounter occurs even without previous voice contact. All that is needed is an address typed on the screen.

Such are the multiple sexual encounters per week of a close friend and collaborator of mine. His behavior causes me anxiety because it isn't premeditated and is therefore risky. In the film based on a novel by Tennessee Williams, *The Roman Spring of Mrs. Stone,* the aging Mrs. Stone, who is a lonely American ex-actress living luxuriously in Rome, despairingly decides to throw her key, wrapped in a handkerchief, down to the scruffy, handsome vagrant who has been trailing her throughout the course of the film. The last images show him in his bedraggled coat ascending the staircase, then, inside her home, lumbering toward her.

24

In the 1950s, when the physical spaces of America were still considered manageable, the quixotic image of a brave little eleven-year-old, dolled up for traveling alone, with a miniature suitcase, was not uncommon. He or she would be led onto the train or bus by a family member and picked up at the other end by the trusted person who was the intention of the visit. The child would have had an adventure and gained a new measure of self-reliance. But today, the image of a child alone in public is one of neglect and impending exploitation. And, accordingly, a public service advertisement on television about child safety on the Internet, called "America Links Up," shows a dazed eleven-year-old middle-class girl wandering alone past the monotonous counters of an airport. A voice asks whether anyone would want their daughter to undergo such an ordeal. A soothing voice then suggests, "Take the trip together," over an image of an entire stiffly smiling family, scrunched in front of a computer video screen. This recommended space for family activity, of course, is more claustrophobic than ever, tighter than the old circle around the television set. Or perhaps the paradigm is that of the family car, with the adult who is holding the mouse as the designated driver.

Nevertheless, there is of yet little that can be done about excluding minors from X-rated interactions on the Internet. Anyone participating in a chat can represent himself as any age he or she desires. You may think that you are conversing with a twenty-five-year old and actually be talking with someone who is thirteen—or ninety. What is more, the Internet is international. Diverse standards of majority and maturity can lead to some bizarre contacts between individuals of different cultures. I have seen listings from men in their twenties who live in Africa or southeast Asia and are complacently looking for meetings with girls aged between twelve and sixteen.

Like it or not, the Internet is replacing the marketplace as an arena of sex education. How many times in the past has an adult confessed that he or she first learned about sex "on the street"? Now that public forum is being replaced by the Internet. In some ways this is probably less dangerous for children than the dangers of physical contact in the past. The liberal ethic encourages parents to educate their children about the birds and the bees. But for almost every individual, real sexual maturity must take place far from the arena of the original oedipal conflict—with peers or even strangers met haphazardly.

25

The ephemeral quality of cyber-contact persists, regardless of the seeming force or vitality of its specific representations. Consider, for example, the following: On June 13, 1998, at 6 a.m. Eastern Standard Time, a live birth was broadcast over the Internet, sponsored by America's Health Network. The reason? A woman, identified only as Elizabeth, said she hoped that the birth of her fourth child would educate prospective mothers worried about the procedure. She also agreed to have her labor induced medically in order to accommodate the advertised start time of the webcast.

Perhaps similarly, there are now millions of personal webcams broadcasting live images day and night on the Internet for no practical reasons. The first to win global recognition was JenniCam, a low-cost surveillance-style web camera installed in the home of a young woman named Jenni who had decided, as a kind of performance art, to document every detail of her very normal lifestyle for anyone who cared to tune in to it on the web. The success of this site, which included nudity and fornication that was not presented as pornography, inspired other disturbingly ordinary young people to begin webcasts. At any hour of the day, one can tune into a host of them and watch their subjects work at their computer, clean house, cook, sleep, shower, study their bodies in the mirror, masturbate, make love, or feed the cat. Over time, the virtual voyeurism of such experiences has a deeply deadening effect upon one's expectations of others. For no matter how long one watches these minimalist Warholian broadcasts, one must succumb to the vacuous feeling that there has been no real encounter. This puts webcam voyeurism on a level below that of the most cursory and coldest encounter imaginable with a street prostitute.

Everything about the age of information conspires toward the ultimate removal of the *private* confession, which, according to Max Weber, accomplished the periodical discharge of the heavy emotional burden of sin that weighed upon the cultures of Christianity. Put in its place, according to Weber, was a Calvinist dialogue with God, which took place constantly and in total isolation. This spiritual isolation, on the other hand, was instrumental in forging the self-reliant Anglo-Saxon mentality, now typified globally by the American entrepreneurial spirit but hopelessly vulgarized by the American management mentality. And the same isolation has reared its head in the at-home spectacle of the Internet, a medium that encourages constant confession and physical solitude.

26

I'm suggesting that promiscuity on the Internet is in some ways another phenomenon of the girdled yet fragmented

Protestant psyche. It is of a piece with children's beauty pageants and the imagination of satanic abuse—a kind of vessel for irresponsible outpourings, projected far from their source out of the necessity to disown them. Meanwhile, in keeping with the Protestant ethic, the individual is essentially alone, wondering if he has been chosen by God or not. Certainly Weber would agree that the narcissistic play of Internet surfing in one way fulfills the Protestant ethic, which stressed a radical focus on the self. As Weber pointed out, all the spiritual biographies of the Protestant movement—in particular, Bunyan's *Pilgrim's Progress*—concentrated on the project of *self*-salvation, which occurred while the seeker momentarily forgot the fates of others.

In a few situations in which Internet fantasy abandons solitude and prompts physical contact, unexpected complications may result. In 1998, a Columbia University graduate student named Oliver Jovanovic was sentenced to fifteen years to life in prison for the kidnapping and sexual assault of a twenty-year-old woman he had met on the Internet. According to Joan Ullman, a journalist who reviewed the case after conviction for the magazine *Psychology Today,* Jovanovic was convicted by a naive judge and jury who, at least in his case, identified Internet postings as simple truth rather than concoctions of sexual fantasy. The legal maneuverings of the prosecution expurgated multiple references to very kinky sex in the victim's e-mail, making use of the rape-shield law, which keeps sex crime victims from being defamed during a trial by barring their past sexual history as evidence. This helped establish the victim as someone who could not have possibly consented to the extended session of violent sex that later occurred in Jovanovic's apartment.

Ullman presented some of the expurgated features of the woman's e-mail, which were available to the public only after the trial. She saw them as typically characteristic of today's sexual cyberculture: "The most important facts include blurring of male and female identities, cocktails of fact and fantasy, sharp disjunctions and free associations in thoughts, and the fluid assumption of new personas, all aided and abetted by hyperfast communication in the absence of verbal and visual cues to behavior."

Using screen names (Jovanovic used "Gray" and the young woman used the French-expletive-derived "Zutzut5"), the couple freely discussed dismemberment, serial killer and cannibal Jeffrey Dahmer, partners devouring each other in science-fiction sex narratives, and other transgressive subjects before meeting in person. At some point during the time when they finally got together in Jovanovic's apartment, Jovanovic tied the woman to his futon chair-bed and allegedly spent twenty hours submitting her to violent sex play, which included gagging and choking, dripping hot candle wax, biting her breasts to the point of bleeding, beating her about the legs and genital area, and sodomizing her. Although Zutzut5 testified that she offered no resistance until the second hour, she claimed this had happened because she was intellectually intimidated by Jovanovic, believed that the sex play would not become that serious and, in general, was not, at the time, a very assertive person. She put off seeking medical help after the incident for several days. She also wrote Jovanovic some e-mails afterwards expressing trauma but including other ambivalent, excited remarks about having a "renewed enthusiasm for life." The defense attorney tried to portray her as a deluded person who had consented to sadomasochistic sex and was now prosecuting Jovanovic to absolve herself of guilt. The prosecutor cast her as a playful person whose fantasies had been forced upon her by a ruthless and deranged sadist. At no point was there an in-depth discussion about the meaning of Internet role-play and its relationship to behavior in other settings.

Ullman portrays this encounter, which, except for one evening, was played out on the Internet, as "a postmodern courtship." She adds that cyberculture "has turned the expression of traditional romantic love into its opposite, converting potential lovers into rival Scheherazades, each trying to top the other with the most sordid and shocking images or ideas."

Eventually, there was a retrial, in which some of the woman's e-mails were admitted as evidence.

I myself have found that Internet sexual encounters, when they remain permanently within that domain—as they often seem to do—provide for radical identities that a person may not even be aware exist inside. In the past, I was able to control my video conferencing to cast myself as one of several types I consider rather alien to me. Soft lighting, using more than two bulbs set at strategic locations, as well as a high-angled camera, sculpt my face to make me look younger and sweeter, and this has attracted and aroused older, more dominant types. Harsh one- or two-bulb lighting, placed in as frontal a position as possible, and including the exposure of certain body parts, casts me as a forbidding and perhaps powerful paternal figure, which seems to attract younger, slimmer, smoother "bottoms" or cubs looking for a bear. I can play either role, depending upon mood—neither of which I can play in person and neither of which have more than a tangential relationship to the hyper verbal, obsessive, warm, ironic, narcissistic, vulnerable personality I believe myself to be in "real" life.

27

<<HEY, ARE YOU AS HOT AS YOUR PROFILE?>> The window had suddenly popped onto my screen as I was answering a professional e-mail. By "profile," the author was referring to that on-screen description logged with America Online, which one can write and make available to all other members—to provide them with information about oneself. (Many people have multiple profiles, one for each screen name.)

I typed in a quick, playful message to the intruder: <<Even hotter. What's it to you?>>

Then I went back to my letter.

But the stranger, whose screen name was UNOUWANIT persisted. <<Then can you handle me?>>

I quickly looked up UNOUWANIT's profile. There was none, so I punched out, <<Handle you? You don't exist.>> Then I closed the chat window, sentencing the encounter to tabula rasa, before going back to my work.

A minute later, the window popped up again. <<I've got better than a profile, baby, a web page. Want to see it?>>

Despite myself, I typed, <<What's the address?>>

The address that UNOUWANIT sent me only brought up an error message. But that screen was superimposed by another message from him or her: <<Like me?>>

Enlivened by an opportunity for verbal sadism, I typed in, <<You're a knockout . . . But I'd suggest a new wig, a visit to the dentist, and a better-looking artificial leg.>>

<<But are you getting hard?>>

<<To tell you the truth all it brought up was an error message.>>

Once again I went back to my letter writing. Then, suddenly, my screen was filled with interjections that galloped across it: <<BRUXE ["BRUXE" is my internet screen name]: Help! Stop doing this!!! I can't stand it anymore! @$%&*!%^&*$#. Let go of me, UNOUWANIT!>> I hadn't typed a thing. <<How did you do that?>> I typed to UNO-UWANIT, astonished.

<<It's a little program I invented>>, he typed back.

My body coursed with excitement. Someone had cracked a major program of the blue-chip company America Online and could control the chat window. The person could make anyone say anything! Attendant to this admiration of UNO-UWANIT's hacking skills was a vague sense of dread that only impelled me farther.

What followed was a verbal sexual encounter in which UNOUWANIT portrayed himself as a small, wiry computer nerd of twenty-six who wanted to make me wild with his descriptions of what we could do physically as well as by the tricks of his programming magic. The encounter had an important element of good sex: it only gets good as you let go and let happen. With UNOUWANIT taking words "out of my mouth" and writing my scenario for me every few replies, our "lovemaking" was a cybernetic roller-coaster ride into his brazen and aggressive reconstruction of my consciousness. <<I can read your mind!>> he typed at one point.

And indeed, he could, for statements popped onto the screen attached to my name one after another without my ever typing.

28

A day later the infection I'd caught from UNOUWANIT began to devastate my hard drive. First the sound in my webcam program began to malfunction, creating bizarre overlaps of audio signals mixed with static. Then my graphics programs refused to open, claiming to have lost essential .DLL files. When I couldn't even open my word processor, I began to fear for my writing. It was only then that it dawned on me that UNOUWANIT had made me his victim.

After consulting other sources, I later found out that whoever was operating under the screen name UNOU-WANIT had probably been able to access my entire hard drive after passing me a Netbus Trojan, almost as if he were sharing my computer on a network. I'd been infected by the Trojan by going to his website. That meant that, at least temporarily, he had free reign with every file on my hard drive, including my passwords, my personal and business letters, my writing, my agenda, my notes and my photos. Meanwhile, the original copies of what he perhaps now possessed were being corroded by a microbe on my hard drive, so in a short time they would no longer be accessible to *me*. In addition, he could use my password to sign in under my identity, intercepting my e-mail and answering it as he saw fit.

Panicking, I erased my entire hard drive and began from scratch with new passwords. Then I had to reinstall the many programs I used. It took a couple of days. But as soon as I discovered that I hadn't lost any of my writing—because I had backed it up just four days before—my anger was replaced by fascination; my imagination obsessively replayed UNOUWANIT's virtual violation of me. Now I was full of a dreadful urge to reexperience a part of UNOUWANIT's power, but with my increased sophistication about the virtual world. I wanted to engage in a deadly virtual tango with him, within the wild fantasy of what it could be like in the flesh and perhaps, in the end, prove myself the master and even the intimate of this criminal. It was almost as if I had entered a relationship. So, in the guise of a warning about legal action, I wrote UNOUWANIT a threatening "love" letter. In it, I promised in-depth investigation and outraged prosecution.

The next day UNOUWANIT and I chatted by Instant Messenger, but this time my words were not commandeered before I typed. He denied playing any part in sending the virus to my computer and claimed that the same thing had happened to him. However, when I tested him concerning details about his physical appearance and even birthday, his answers matched everything that his supposed impostor had said.

Unfortunately, the hacker seems to have forwarded the IP address of my computer to a database, giving others potential access to my hard drive whenever I am online. I have had to install a firewall, which sets off a siren and blocks entry of anyone trying to enter my hard drive with this stolen number. Then, it tries to trace the perpetrator's path through the Internet, so that he or she can be identified. This alarm goes off an average of two or three times a week on my computer, as new Internet terrorists try to gain access to my virtual brain.

29

The stealing, reuse, fragmenting, and disposal of information now occurring on the Internet smacks of Lyotard's description in *Libidinal Economy* of a world that shifts as our emotions do, electric snakings of libidinal energy and intangible information that bypass rational boundaries and lose historical legitimacy. Like primitive impulses passing through the living brain, public space is now a coil of wavering light that can disappear in a millisecond. The communion of consciousness on the Internet is promiscuous and unpredictable. It finds its model in the idea of purified contact and disclosure, that state of unhampered, immediate communion between the Protestant and his God. But it follows complex rhythms that resemble random, physical encounters on a city street.

The miniature acts of terrorism I have just described intrigued me partly as symptoms of the fact that we are moving toward not a watertight Orwellian 1984 in which only the powers that be have all the data but a Gibsonian future of virtual rapists, unintentional data leaks, schoolboyish terrorist attacks and chaotic mumblings in virtual super-space—not an information vault but an information sieve. The Web is porous and full of loopholes and chances for rule breaking. We are moving, then, toward a new architectural model of experience. Some of it resembles that of the old city.

In fact, virtual architecture is coming more and more to resemble the public space of the city now being abandoned.

Just like traditional downtown, it is a place of fleeting, sometimes dangerous encounters, where the more powerful or more rich or more skillful are devising secure firewalls to protect their resources from the rabble, but where the average pedestrian careens toward unpredictable meetings. This "vicarious geography," as the philosopher Fredric Jameson might call it, is a marsh of vagaries and fantasies and false interactions. And the fact that it is may very well offer hope for the future. On the other hand, sophisticated encryption methods on the part of powerful corporations may lead to the monolithic class divisions of yesteryear. As software guru Peter Upton explained to me, in the case of the control of commerce and communication by large corporations, we may well be moving toward "the clear, amniotic gel of pure encryption" so that no one will be able to break the encoding of their transactions. During a business transaction with a powerful company, we will temporarily bathe in a stream of totally intelligible exchange. But outside of this privileged exchange, our communication will appear to be meaningless babble to potential eavesdroppers. Upon leaving the transaction, we are returned to the dangerous, vulgar world of Internet Populis, where cyber-pickpockets and petty hackers will try to make us their prey.

30

Virtual space copies the physical space of the past. In the past, the complex opportunities of the urban community depended not so much upon law and order as upon loopholes. For this reason, pleasure in all the great cities has come from a vaticanical model. Talk as we may about the growth of the merchant class and the Protestant ethic, until recently cities have in many ways reflected a Catholic sensibility like the Church before the Reformation, fueled by indulgences, graft, Jesuitical deal-making, and the impotence or goofing off of its highest figureheads. Beyond these machinations, another part of the city ran itself on the level of the street. As a result, New York, the century's most interesting American city, eventually became famous for its chaos. Chance advantage, obsessive work, illicit pleasures, architectural decay, and the unofficial deal were characteristic of its circulatory system. The bachelor, the homosexual, the addict, and the unmarried woman were typical and traditional protagonists of urban libido, assuming their identities only within the city's streets.

Obviously, the street is the opposite of the family circle because its population avoids or subverts such a tight structure. From this condition were created the labyrinthine subcultures of pleasure and fleeting interaction that defied the simplifying politics of the nuclear family.

Families never created interesting public spaces. Strangers always did. The hunger and Eros of the uprooted designed the unwholesomely vital sidewalks outside this room in which I now sit naked with the image of YOUNG WANT OLD.

Public Space, Last Gasps

I

1992. The Web is a few years away but Times Square is already headed for a massive renovation. Rudolf Giuliani, the city's new mayor, a man with the rigid, down-turned lips of a corpse, whose suits resemble those of an undertaker, is about to be inaugurated. His physical appearance is the polar opposite of that of his generic political rival, new president William Jefferson Clinton, humanized by his red nose and mawkish smile.

During Mayor Giuliani's inauguration, which is broadcast on television, his chubby, rather larvic-looking son peeks repeatedly from behind his father's back, gloating for the cameras. A decade ago, such Romper Room indulgences would have been an embarrassment for any city official. But during this ceremony they become a brazen declaration of the supreme hegemony of the breeding population. From the moment of his inauguration, Giuliani—unlike the family-less ex-mayor Koch or the discreetly married ex-mayor Dinkins—will belligerently and surgically turn this city into a theme park of family values.

2

Last gasps of the city of pleasure. If the paradise of intergenerational bonding was the utopian desire that impelled certain activists of the sixties, inter*class* bonding is the secret vice that has never left the closet of the cities. There are a paucity of documents in nonfiction and fiction that describe the soon-to-be-extinct urban interactions of the street prostitute and the middle-class john, the sailor and the Ivy League homosexual or the nurse's aide and the physician. With the shrinking of public space and the infinite expansion of virtual space, such encounters, which depend upon subtle physical and linguistic cues, are bound to become more infrequent.

The twenty-six-year-old I met that night in 1992 in a bar about to be closed by Giuliani's morality squad was the type that seemed to have been turning me on since the early eighties. He had a lean, high-cheekboned face that carried a full, curvaceous mouth. His eyes were much too big. They were fixed in a blank yet mean vulnerability.

This is the kind of visage associated in its older versions with frontal photos on WANTED bulletins, or in its younger ones with the heart-shaped snouts of cartoon bad boys, who run wild with Disney's version of Pinocchio to a candy-cane amusement park, before being turned into abused jackasses. He had been coming to Times Square since the age of thirteen and was well aware that his act was getting old. His old-fashioned hand swipes, erotic sneers, and brazen, casual crotch displays were almost obsolete, for they had originally been honed to compliment the much more common urban tango of hustler and john. In my life, the tradition stretched all the way back to adolescence, when I, too, had practiced its dance steps on my trip across country. For this boy, they were a sole talent for livelihood.

This was, however, the last hustler bar in Manhattan, and even it was changing to appeal to a different kind of clientele. Once this boy lost his audience, as the streets of the marketplace were rolled up to make way for the age of information, he and his skills were likely to be dispersed into that sprawling donut-shaped ghetto that already surrounds European cities like Paris and that is rapidly forming around New York. Then there would be little chance for him to fix me in the brazen glare of his eyes or use his thigh to pin me against the bar where we stood talking.

Of course, my interest in young men such as this one who now ran a comb through his licorice strips of hair had really started years before. During an alienated adolescence in the suburbs, I'd stashed away a libidinal imago of this type of boy from other neighborhoods, close to the city center, met on visits to the train station near downtown. There was one boy in particular, who taught me to smoke. When I finally brought this dropout home, my liberal parents hired him to work on my father's car, but he ended up feeling cheated by my father and poured sugar in the gas tank, which destroyed the fuel injection system, and got him shipped permanently back to his underclass neighborhood.

3

I invited the young man from Times Square back to my apartment. After a suspiciously long visit to the bathroom, he came out and sat close to me on my leather couch. He told me that the hair on my forearm reminded him of a doctor's. He even grazed it with callused fingers. Outside of tricks, doctors were one of the few kinds of white professionals with whom the boy was likely to have had memorable contact. There'd undoubtedly been by-the-book social workers and curt lawyers, as well as aggressive cops and correctional officers who'd stripped, herded, or punched him. But these memories were crowded into a dark place with other narratives of abuse. He'd probably chanced upon a doctor in a clinic who'd shown a few moments of gentle concern and laid a soothing hand on his abdomen while probing for an enlarged liver. Then the boy's eyes had rested for a moment upon the sprout of hair on the scrubbed white arm.

Ironically, despite my feeling of triumph in having accomplished a dangerous encounter to ward off my dread of the coming tyranny of the Giuliani administration's family values, this youth reached into his baggy pants and brought out his own family pictures: a girlfriend, a baby daughter. Then he asked me to put on a videotape of heterosexual porn. As he approached my bed with the main objective of earning money, he began to babble about an out-of-date karate film; and then his rumpled clothing peeled away to reveal homemade tattoos and scars: souvenirs, perhaps, of polymorphous events that had occurred in housing projects, holding pens, stairwells, or peepshows.

This time, however, I wasn't prepared for the emaciated body that snaked from the baggy clothes. Was it crack, AIDS? He was lean beyond imagining. It wasn't repulsive but bordered instead on something majestic, appalling. In the beige light coming from the lampshade, his hairless body was a steel cage covered by a thin layer of butter. The only extra flesh lay in his ass cheeks: two grapefruits set into the pelvic bone. Dramatizing this economy was the fact that his body was permanently tensed for combat. Now it sprang forward and enlaced my bulk. Something clicked. My thicker body intuitively filled each hollow. I gave in, letting my legs fall farther and farther apart.

4

It was becoming clearer that the peculiar interclass world of Times Square prostitution was changing. Rumors about the murders of several johns started circulating. They centered around a white boy named Frankie, whom I had tricked with and who had left his winter coat in my closet, never returning for it. On our one evening together, I remember being struck by what I had interpreted as his sociopathic brilliance. During our entire conversation, he seemed to anticipate remarks I was about to make before I even made them. It was a nimble and gloating reading of my mentality that I have seldom encountered. Come to think of it, it was a real-life version of the Internet chat violation I have described above. Frankie had developed a program for putting words into my mouth. It scared me. Although he called about the coat and made another date to see me, I felt a certain relief when he didn't show up.

Later information about Frankie came from "Pearl," a loquacious black accessories designer who always used this female moniker for the street. According to Pearl, Frankie had multiple personalities. He was a heroin addict—a macho and ruthless homeboy who was constantly acquiring property from tricks and then abandoning it at the next location. His persona could swing wildly from ghetto bravado to a gay sensibility full of "Miss Thing"s. Once in a heated discussion with Pearl, he had extracted a large hunting knife from his pants. Apparently, this knife had recently taken the lives of three johns in succession.

The story about Frankie's serial killings circulated for several weeks. Little by little, they sank into the mired obscurity of all Times Square gossip. One never hears the real version of a violent incident, or even knows for certain whether it actually occurred. Such depressing stories inhibit the smooth functioning of the underworld subculture. Eventually, they are dismissed as bad dreams so that life can go on.

5

Soon after the talk of Frankie the hustler's homicides faded, Times Square's last hustler bar finished its renovations, to keep up with the changes in the neighborhood. Slowly and almost imperceptibly, most of the homeboys were replaced by another brand of prostitute. Wanting a higher echelon, the Irish American owner from Hell's Kitchen, who had supported Giuliani even when her bar was considered a blight on Times Square, kept the old hustlers out by a variety of strategies. She instituted a five-dollar entrance charge, designed to discourage crack heads who would spend their last buck on a toke; she banned anyone who went in and out of the bar several times within one evening; and she invented instantaneous dress codes—no baseball cap or no tank top, or anything that an undesirable happened to be wearing that evening. It only worked for a while. Today there are no hustler bars in Manhattan.

6

A few months later, the antiporn zoning law that the Giuliani administration had been pushing finally went through. It specified that stores with more than 40 percent X-rated material and theaters or clubs that featured erotic dancing could not operate within five hundred feet of a residence, school, or place of worship. This ruled out practically the entire island of Manhattan, which has apartments or lofts even in the forlorn warehouse areas near the river. As a result, using a strategy that I found fraught with delicious irony, some of the sex shops began featuring souvenirs for tourists, cheap electrical products and G-rated books in their windows. Careful to ensure that the X-rated merchandise represented less than 40 percent of their merchandise, they piled it into the back of the store. Naive tourists arriving in family groups sometimes took the bait and entered—and then, once they had made it past the low-quality merchandise up front, found themselves and their children surrounded by pornography.

For the working force of male and female erotic dancers, the situation proved more complicated. During a period of about two weeks, dozens of go-go and lap-dancing clubs throughout the city were suddenly raided and padlocked. Dancers who had depended upon the X-rated industry for years suddenly found themselves unemployed. Some establishments stayed open, but according to the new ruling, both the breasts of women and the genitals and buttocks of women and men had to be covered.

7

At the hustler bar I have just described, which had go-go boys in the basement, these restrictions led, at least temporarily, to new and ingenious artifices. The male dancers designed bathing suits that had unusual codpieces. They would cut a hole in the crotch and then sew on a sack designed from the same material in the shape of a penis. Their penis fitted into this cloth shaft, which could also be stuffed with padding to look bigger. The back of the bathing suit had a seam that pulled the material inside the division of the buttocks. These outfits looked a lot more obscene than the backless thongs the dancer had worn before the ruling. In addition, the dancers devised erotic pantomimes on stage that were both aesthetically advanced and obscenely suggestive. These would be met by thunderous applause.

8

It wasn't so much the assault on eroticism in New York as the new prohibition against interclass interaction that really depressed me. One by one, Bronx and Brooklyn homeboys whom I had known since the early eighties started disappearing from street corners and bars. Some had become ill, but others had been arrested or had given up because of the lack of business and disappeared into ghettoes that were exclusively populated by their kind. One of the last havens of sleaze in Times Square—the only place where drag queens were welcome—had been raided by the police after a drug investigation of several months. Its door remained padlocked and bore a large orange police sticker that explained the charges: prostitution and drug trafficking. The orange sticker further notified the reader that anyone removing it would be subject to arrest. On a particularly depressing evening I stood reading it with Paulie, a razor-thin, highly verbal homeboy with a gun hobby, whom I had known and liked since I'd first been a john. In a joint impulse Paulie and I used our fingernails to pry up opposite corners of the sticker. Then we galloped down the block with the shredded official document, just as a cop was rounding the corner.

9

In the past I have written a great deal about dangerous encounters with those who could not be socialized. But as the normalizing machine of commerce gobbles up public space,

57

I now admit that the energies of the id have fled to a less substantial realm. The *Psychopathia Sexualis* of Krafft-Ebing is no longer a stroll through a neighborhood of live monsters, but electric energy brought into our consciousness by the tap of a keyboard. We have stopped locating perversity in the corporeal other, and because of this the romanticized narrative of the criminal may be ending. *Noir*—the titillating vampirism of class difference—may be over. Instead, we ourselves are the ones who cannot really be socialized, even if such a fact exists only on the plane of the imagination.

Like dull automatons in a cheap science fiction film, our bodies continue to go through the requisite motions of hygiene, work and procreation, moving themselves from point A to point B. Meanwhile, our minds spit our longings and obscenities into the atmosphere. And media have ensured that these ejaculations are everywhere. The self is now nowhere in particular, and, depending upon how you look at it, we have everywhere, or nowhere, to go.

Several texts from very diverse sources provided inspiration and/or information for this essay. They include Bill Andriette's "Dumbed Down and Played Out: The Gay Movement and the Liquidation of Boy Love" and Jesse Green's "The Men from the Boys," in *Taking Liberties,* ed. Michael Bronski (New York: Masquerade Books, 1996); Harry Hay's and Will Roscoe's writings in *Radically Gay,* ed. Will Roscoe (Boston: Beacon Press, 1996); Lawrence Wright's *Remembering Satan: A Tragic Case of Recovered Memory* (New York: Vintage, 1994); Max Weber's *The Protestant Ethic and*

the Spirit of Capitalism, translated by Talcott Parsons (repr. New York: Routledge, 1992); and Philippe Aries's *Centuries of Childhood,* translated by Robert Baldick (London: J. Cape, 1962).

I'm grateful to Ursule Molinaro and Chris Farrell for pointing me toward some of my ideas.

Surrendering
to the Spectacle

$\Bigl[\ ^{M}\Bigr]$y question is: When did art and entertainment go their separate ways? For, to be honest, I've always relied on art as the fundamental link between intellect and pleasure. The politicization in recent years of questions surrounding this link has, for me, nearly destroyed what is fascinating about art, substituting instead suspicion, cynicism, and puritanical prohibitions for what could be force, relevance, and intense pleasure. I'll admit a feeling on my part that the manipulation of mass media in the art world in such a *conscious* way (i.e., conceptually), for the purpose of social commentary, has produced a new kind of arid elitism, in what was formerly art's most sensual domain—the plastic arts. The targets of my bitterness are, obviously, a large proportion of the conceptual, appropriationist, and neo-situationist, overtly politicized productions.

Theories of the Spectacle as a covert apparatus of social control have developed, in my opinion, into harbingers of an even more heinous sort of social and aesthetic control. And many of those artists and critics who claim to be working to subvert the power of the Spectacle appear as little more than purveyors of that same stiff-necked backlash that chastised Wordsworth for his fascination with the popular ballad, an interest that was neither ironic nor critical. More than being warriors against the Spectacle and its economic control, these new critics are, if I may be so bold as to say, envious that the cultures and classes into which they were born and educated, or into which they have struggled for entrance, are no longer the cultures of the classes that own *entertainment.* They are then jealous of pleasure and are on a self-righteous crusade to annihilate it.

I find the most obsessive critics of the Spectacle generally the most drained of libidinous energy, and thus deprived of real entertainment. I go so far as to point to the personality and biography of Guy Debord—father of the theory of the Spectacle—as symptomatic of a dour, paranoid mentality that is obsessed with issues of the super-ego. Additionally, I think that if the Spectacle actually is a hypnotic means of social control, its critics would best seek to subvert it by exaggerating, rather than trying to excise, its energy and vulgarity.

The exaltation of the vulgar was rampant in the "prepolitical" (or "pre-Stonewall") male homosexual sensibility to which I still avidly subscribe. An obsession with popular entertainment, especially film, kept me—and a small coterie of much more well-known homosexual artists (Jack Smith, Kenneth Anger, Andy Warhol, Rudi Geinrich, Manuel Puig, John Waters) as well as countless stylists, clothing designers, hairdressers, film fans, and others of us who draw, in a desperate manner, sustenance from their imaginations—vital and aware.[1] In the midst of doomlike pronouncements about the media and a semiotics of cultural control, as well as the decay of these pronouncements into empty knee-jerk gestures on the part of many artists, academics, and cultural critics, we were able to continue to draw meaning and originality from entertainment. But how?

We did it by *excess.* For what Bataille realized, and those who work in the legacy of Debord have forgotten, is that an excess of entertainment, an overload of pleasure in its greedy, promiscuous, orgiastic sense, becomes an archetypal celebration of the energies of the human tribe, a vehicle for emotional exploration and transformation. Thus, we perverts consumed popular culture in the sense of devouring it. As promiscuous people, we sought an Eden of the appetite and of imagination. Our main goal in life was to be entertained.

This compulsion for entertainment on the part of certain of us male homosexuals was perfectly in line with a compulsion to Hollywoodize life, a tendency reinforced again and again by our exclusion from and alienation by the nonentertainment aspects of society (schools, families, communities) and by the libidinal rewards of having dicks in our mouths. And since this willful submersion in fantasy, in the world of the imagination—films, colors, clothes, design, dicks—could be repeated ad infinitum, we lived, or tried to live, in an eternal Paradise.

Our overflowing state of mind had no need of a dialectic to loosen the bonds of social control because it was so *excessive.* Mere appetite and a controlled gag reflex were enough for the creation of a truly alternative consciousness. If messages in the media around us were designed to manipulate us, our devouring of them transformed them by a kind of violent digestion. It was a delirium that never could have been induced by high culture, community ideals, or socially sanctioned sex.

I can illustrate how a taste for pleasure devoured constraints by describing the way I, barely an adolescent, felt on my first visit to seedy Times Square, in the early 1960s. The harsh lights, oversized signs, smell of burning flesh from the hotdog stand, ringed eyes of pallid prostitutes, black-and-white male cheesecake magazines, outlines of genitals through the Mod pants of hustlers, stench of the homeless, grimy pant cuffs of the speed dealers, and the runaways— with their bruised arms—might have been semiotic signs; but all that they spelled was a liberating gibberish, a story of chaos. These symbols of appetite gone wild and evil were the forest in which I found congress with the dislocated. And these were still the days when many homosexuals, not at all assimilated, found a haven in the world of thieves, prostitutes, and other rejects.

What an incredible time we had! And what an incredible role cheap entertainment played in our avoidance of social prohibitions. The theaters on Times Square's 42nd Street were open twenty-four hours a day. Some played first-run or last year's features at a discount, on a triple bill. But once you entered you were in another kind of story world, one whose characters were the lonely and the unmarried, the criminal, the homeless, or the sexual deviant—their world a kind of self-service Hollywood. I remember my first whiff of the decaying interiors of these cavernous, deco-era theaters—mildew, heated celluloid, floor wax. No one looked askance at someone arriving in the middle of a film, then staying to see the beginning, because the plot of the film wasn't the point. Its cosmology was. You entered it the way you enter a hypnotic trance, without paying much conscious attention to it. It was a drug. And once the social outsider had entered the altered state, color, music, images—always at a remove—became his landscape. You were, in the most radical sense, *escaping the world.*

At first, there is only pitch-blackness, as the eyes, having come from the blinding light of the street into the theater, grow accustomed to the darkness. Then slowly, as a stale odor fills the nostrils, fuzzy forms are visible here and there in the seats, mostly single figures, males, some who look transfixed into a kind of depression, others who are snoozing, still others who peer through the darkness with squinted eyes, looking in every direction. In the balcony, the distribution of forms is different: small knots of people, an occasional gasp or smacking sound, a rustling like the sound of scurrying rats.

After I have stumbled into a seat, the light from the screen floods my eyes. A color film. Several years old, its Technicolor is already fading. That first time it was, I remember, Stanley Donen's *Seven Brides for Seven Brothers,*[2] a musical of rural sex segregation and taboo breaking. In the film, seven women are trapped in a mountain ranch by an avalanche and by a group of boisterous cowboys who want to court them.

A couple of hours pass, as the brain enters the dwarfed labyrinth of the unreal narrative. Its constraints are an invitation to forge a new identity and a new self. Then slowly, an increasing number of scratches in the image mean that the last reel is near the end. The viewer surfaces partially from his trance as another film begins: an elegant costume drama meant to be taking place in French Canada.[3] It seems that a scientist has invented a device that can dissolve and then reconstitute living matter. Upstairs, his attractive wife cares for their child. But in the basement, the scientist is preparing to test his device. He steps into a glass compartment and pulls a lever that starts the process. His body is dissolved and sent a few feet through space to another glass compartment, where it becomes reconstituted; however, he has failed to notice the fly that had gotten into the first compartment with him. His body is reconstituted with the fly's head and one of its legs for a hand. What a grotesque metaphor for Canada's double cultural identity! Now his elegant, horrified wife begins searching for the transformed fly with the miniature head of a man, which is buzzing around the garden or in the house.

Bathed in this irreal world, your eyes grow blank once again, the limbs become heavy, anesthetized, in a receptive, hypnotic trance, which erases all anxiety, as the form sitting a few seats away shifts over, seat by seat, until he is sitting next to you. Then, as if by chance, a knee falls casually against yours. And as your eyes dive into the false gothic luxury of the scientist's wife's dresses and the furnishings of their French Canadian house, or the repulsive but thrilling image of animal and man changing heads, you feel grateful for the warmth of the stranger's body pressing ever more insinuatingly against yours; for a moment you look away from the screen and take in his fixed, aroused face in the dim light of the theater, as his hand slides down your chest in a fumbling caress and finds the opening of your fly, and his fingers, nervous and hot, grasp your genitals. And then, almost noiselessly, he slides off his seat onto his knees and wedges his head between your thighs, and the rise and fall of desire is undercut by, then bolstered by, and finally one with the shifting colors, lights, and patterns of the film on the screen, the rush toward its nauseating, touching climax.

Tomes have already been written about the male homosexual mechanism of identification with melodrama. Like Manuel Puig, who would later write *Kiss of the Spider Woman*—in which the illusions of two Argentine prisoners, a revolutionary and a pederast, are stripped bare by the force of each other's political identities—many other artistic homosexual men have found that the conservative clichés of Hollywood are a source of transforming irony, a subversive way of cross-gender identification that liberates them, temporarily anyway, from the rules of their oppressive community. No need to delve into the well-known examples of Andy Warhol, Jack Smith, or John Waters here. But the brilliant syntheses of high and low culture accomplished by Manuel Puig merit consideration, for not only did he reveal the deep political rewards of the creative use of pop entertainment, he also found his fantasies in the network of cheap movie theaters and sordid hotels that made up Times Square in the sixties and seventies.

In *Kiss of the Spider Woman*, the effeminate homosexual turns the jail cell he shares with a heterosexual revolutionary into a seraglio where tales woven from Hollywood films create a true politics of marginality, simplicity, and sacrifice.

By the end of the book, the homosexual becomes the sacrificial female heroine, as he agrees to carry a dangerous message to the revolutionary's contact outside the prison. As a person who identified in his deepest consciousness with female concerns, Manuel himself was able, partly unconsciously, to create a dynamic politics of culture. This wedding of Marxist values and homoerotic sentimentality is radical; for, rather than building a critique of the Spectacle from outside, it enters its treacherous hall of mirrors with enough abandon, enough courage, and enough originality to resignify its meanings. Finding liberation in female stereotypes, La Puig also found a solution to the tyranny of the Spectacle.

With our immersion in entertainment, how did we faggots manage to reconcile the glamour of film with the sleazy elements of our lives? On 42nd Street between 8th and 9th Avenues was a ramshackle hotel catering to transients. After an inexpensive evening of watching reruns of Garbo languishing in expensive clothes against velvet furniture, La Puig, like myself, sometimes combed the streets for sex. And if the hero that he lured was somewhat less couth than the leading man, or if their love nest smelled too strongly of antiseptic or unchanged sheets, the intoxicating act of anonymous sex, the dizzy risk of giving in to the active, largely unknown partner, suddenly pulled Manuel into a whirling vortex of signifiers, a world beyond narratives and politics that cannot be deconstructed by judgments about or criticisms of the cultural clichés he manipulated to bring about this experience. To say that Puig did not actually reach the sublime heights of ecstasy and elegance promised by the most hackneyed film plot would be dishonestly to deny him his creative power. And this power, armed with fantasies of intoxicated surrender, was also a tool of cultural criticism.

By the mid-sixties, films on 42nd Street came less often from the gaudy Hollywood machine. Another genre was developing.[4] It was lower than the B film, in its early stages it was shot in black and white, and it presented transgressive subjects as a kind of sleazy entertainment. Because of limits imposed by censorship laws, these exploitation films,[5] featuring big-breasted actresses, out-of-work New York actors suffering from heroin addiction or alcoholism, working-class directors eager to make a quick buck, and screenwriters familiar with underground cinema, had an enticing quality of marginality. The films dealt with sex, addiction, and violence and ranged from the gently comic to the horrifically atrocious. Straining against the repressive laws of the time, they had to rely much more heavily on story than today's pornography. They gave me a real taste for urban noir precisely because of their stunted production values, the strange subcultures they revealed.

I remember sitting transfixed in a darkened theater as, onscreen, in black and white, two actors, a man and a woman, writhed half naked on rumpled sheets in a dimly lit hotel room. In this scene, he was going through heroin withdrawal, and she was trying to keep him from taking another injection by arousing him in a way so frankly sexual for the time that the viewer could not doubt the absurd premise of the power of her body over the demands of his addiction.

Because these films invented a freaky half-world of sin that couldn't go far enough in exploiting the atrocities of this world, they were some of the most sublime aesthetic (or, should I say, *synthetic*) experiences I have ever had. No matter that they were often prefaced by a scene in which a doctor explained to the audience that the film was being presented merely for educational purposes. This ludicrous element, including the hackneyed plots, only added to the trance state produced by such vehicles, whose only real purpose was to arouse and titillate. Our own dream worlds are no less stunted nor less devoid of convincing naturalistic elements.

A great moment in cultural irony occurred when a theater that normally played such B films decided to give Andy Warhol's film *My Hustler* (1965) a brief run. I went to see it. An audience dulled by hangovers, homelessness, or sex binges sat mutely in front of the screen, slightly confused by the fact that they were not being offered the usual B fare. However, *My Hustler* is so derivative of the exploitation films of the period that it almost passed. As the film played on, I began to sense a vague rapport between the bohemians who had come to see the film and the usual 42nd Street crowd, proving that art can succeed in being experimental without being elitist.

I come from a later era than Manuel Puig, when the quest for sensation took on a less clandestine but more dangerous cast. I remember some of the films playing on 42nd Street after I returned to New York in 1974 and much of the block had been claimed by hardcore sex shops—namely, two atrocity films, *Ilsa: She Wolf of the SS* (1975, dir. Don Edmonds), which was a sequel to *Olga's House of Shame;* and, ten years later, Ruggero Deodato's *Cannibal Holocaust* (1985), one of the most horrifying films of carnage ever made. Of course, there were plenty of hardcore porno films by that time as well. Although these films were more disturbing than the gentle perversities I'd seen upon first arriving in Times Square, they produced the same trance experience. Their sensationalism was apolitical, ill meaning, and thus truly subversive—Sadean carnage as an answer to repressive order.

Around the corner from the theater where *Ilsa* was playing was the Haymarket, a cavernous, seedy hustler bar with a subculture so full of colorful characters that it formed the basis for the renowned off-Broadway play *Forty-Deuce*.[6] By now, hardcore drugs had taken over Times Square's subcultures, and risky sexual encounters with drug-addicted machos were a weird complement to the sensational rituals of dismemberment and cannibalism taking place onscreen. In the men's room of the theater, the early sixties' furtive loner, single gentleman, or boy from Brooklyn had given way to Tod Browning's gallery of players from *Freaks* (1932). There were gold-toothed dealers, one-armed hustlers, grime-covered runaways, retarded janitors, and transvestite prostitutes, all shaped by the saga of extreme poverty. The violence quotient had increased.

Today's critics of entertainment, with their anodyne interpretations of the power of pleasure, would deduce from such a change that the spectacle offered by Times Square had been lowered to exploitation's common denominator. But I'm seeking in this essay to redefine entertainment partly as risk, as overflowing, as a chance to penetrate social barriers. Just as identification with the female heroines of films liberated some male homosexuals dissatisfied with the opportunities for identity within their communities, and just as the irreality of the films playing in these theaters, interwoven with that of anonymous sexual contacts taking place in the seats, became a cauldron for creativity, so did the later influx of drifters into Times Square expand chances for libidinal experience and experiments with class. When the surgeon adopted the street urchin and the professor fell in love with the hustler, class structures were temporarily subverted; order was challenged.

However, the interface of drug-world addiction and homosexual desire that played itself out in Times Square in the seventies and eighties soon became a dance of death punctuated by new diseases (AIDS) and new drugs (crack). Pleasure became a question of life and death. The fact that the search for entertainment (in the sense in which I have been defining it) was carried on under these conditions re-defines entertainment as something more essential, even as something metaphysical, for despite its potential ultimate cost, people would not abandon it.

The Puerto Rican family of brothers I found hanging out in front of a hustler bar in the mid-eighties (after the Hay-market had closed) had come to Times Square in a chain re-action. As each reached adolescence, he found himself in conflict with his alcoholic mother and her current boyfriend. Each boy became a runaway and was, in turn, initiated to Times Square by the next-older brother. There was also a half-sister, who had hit the streets at fourteen and been picked up by a disciple of Gurdjieff more than forty years her senior, who succeeded in keeping her off the drug angel dust and off the streets by a series of pregnancies and the power of infinite patience.

When experiments with promiscuity and Hollywood fantasy were beginning to go stale, I met this family of vagrants, and, little by little, they began to take over my apartment. There were unpredictable visits that resulted in mattresses and sleeping bags covering every spare inch of the floor, an occasional attempt to camp out in my hallway when I wasn't home. There were drug crises that left me with a young charge who was babbling and hallucinating, a case of gonorrhea caught by the youngest, who needed me to take him to a clinic. There was a VCR theft that had neighbors, who became familiar with the brothers when they shouted up to my window, worried and suspicious. And for me there were day-to-day lessons on the exotic, incestuous, treacherous sociology of an impoverished Latino brotherhood. They initiated me into a deeper knowledge of the power of entertainment and its darker consequences, imparted a mentality to me that taught me how to cope with what Times Square had become. They were also the first in a string of ever-riskier involvements, as I began to focus my libidinal energies more and more obsessively on underclass life.

This new form of entertainment—what should I call it? "live entertainment"? "high-risk entertainment"? I call it entertainment not to sound flippant but because its very hard-core nature turned me into a spectator. I could participate in the lives of the Puerto Rican brothers, marvel and tremble and cringe, but I would never live them. This entertainment was a kind of Russian roulette perfectly in line with the times and with the fact that an attack on the imagination was taking place. The urgency of urban decay, the end of the sexual revolution, AIDS, feminism: together they were a bugle call to grim reality, an attempt to announce the end of entertainment, a disapproving judgment of the overweening fantasy life that had made prepolitical male homosexual artists so compelling and so promiscuous, so socially irresponsible from an unimaginative point of view.

Nevertheless, there would be no stopping some of us who championed the trance and the tyranny of the sensory. Our flight from community norms, if it was to continue, had to become more perverse, and more dangerous. My successive experiments with street drugs, and my increasing familiarity with criminals were nothing more than a search for imaginative material. It was at this time that I discovered a principle—worthwhile entertainment is an assault on identity; the pleasure it provides is in direct proportion to its transformative powers, to its threat.

When Times Square was renovated in the mid-1990s, a power greater than the imagination took over that space. Behind the greed of the investors and the expansion of the Disney Corporation, behind the call to law and order of citizens outraged by the pornography, drugs, and violence, was a deep disillusionment with free play, with the pleasures of chaos as it used to play out in the urban scene. The renovation of Times Square was, then, an attempt to bring the predictability and conformity of suburban American life to the city.

Unbelievably, there was a short period when the vacated theaters and storefronts of 42nd Street, waiting for renovation, were turned over to conceptual artists who decorated marquees and storefronts. This tepid restatement of urban libido was maddening to me, simply for the fact that it was unwittingly helping accomplish the transformation of

Times Square from the spontaneous to the contrived, from the *felt* to the *thought out*. Obviously, the conceptual artists who were part of this project before the renovation thought they had found a terrific opportunity for irony. And some of them doubtlessly valued the energies of old Times Square. But their appropriation of pop culture in the service of sociopolitical criticism or postmodern "haiku" failed to do justice to the hypnotic power of the Spectacle that old Times Square had celebrated.

Now the new Times Square—with its theme restaurants, multiplex film complexes, and souvenir stores—purports to be solely about entertainment, but free play and risk have been replaced by tourist buses and packs of families. At the very moment when the triumph of a new middle class has been working to make our pleasures anodyne by removing their vital connection to true vulgarity, those of us who were willing to die for pleasure—in the most literal sense—are seldom heard.

Notes

1. Jack Smith, who made the film *Flaming Creatures* (1963), died of AIDS in 1989. Kenneth Anger, maker of underground films, including *Scorpio Rising* (1964), wrote the most notorious of the Hollywood scandal books, *Hollywood Babylon*. Andy Warhol's diary is mostly gossip. Rudi Geinrich began as an early gay liberationist, but became famous as the first designer to bare the female breast in bathing suits and evening gowns. Manuel Puig kept a library of more than four thousand videotaped films, which he watched with his mother daily. John Waters collects mementoes about mass murderers.

2. *Seven Brides for Seven Brothers* (1954, dir. Stanley Donen). John Woo cites this movie as one of his inspirations for his violence-ballets.

3. *The Fly* (1958, dir. Kurt Neumann).

4. For example: *Scum of the Earth* (1963, dir. Herschell Gordon Lewis), *One Shocking Moment* (1965, dir. Ted V. Mikels), *Olga's House of Shame* (1964, dir. Joseph Mawra), *The Agony of Love* (1965, dir. William Rotsler), *A Taste of Flesh* (1967, dir. Doris Wishman a.k.a. Lou Silverman), *Orgy at Lil's Place* (1963, dir. Jerald Intrator), *Mondo Bizarro* (1966, dir. Lee Frost).

5. Perhaps the only filmmaker of this genre to later come into prominence was Russ Meyer, who specialized in comic adult films. The entire genre came and went in a few years, as censorship laws were relaxed. Until recently, the genre was barely remembered. Now, such films are becoming fetishized by the lovers of the marginal.

6. *Forty-Deuce* (1981) was written by Alan Bowne. In 1982 it was made into a film, unreleased, by Paul Morrissey.

Fear of Fashion

Dressed as he was, in indifference to the winter weather and current trends, the Puerto Rican youth still looked stunning. I stood in a subway car, gazing at his gleaming black hair, cut Caesar-style, combed forward at the front and sides. Each cluster of bangs along his forehead came to a perfect filigreed point, whose tip was bleached nearly platinum white. Conversely, the hair at the back feathered into only one inverted triangle, which twisted coquettishly into a single curl against the soft, tobacco-colored skin of a strong neck.

He had softened his prominent, almost Neanderthal brow ridges by razor-nicking a series of vertical lines along each of his eyebrows, turning them into two barcodes. These complemented the shadow of a goatee, shaved to pencil-line proportions around pouting lips and a dimpled chin.

His T-shirt was of black net, revealing the shadow of nipples and striped vertically by two violet suspenders, which held up baggy, zoot-suit trousers. However, the most astonishing elements of his dress were his accessories: thick fake-gold and silver rings encircling three of the stout fingers of one hand, several ropes of gold plate hanging from his neck, an enormous green rhinestone sprouting from the lobe of each ear. His was, unmistakably, a kind of dandyism, a street version that only accentuated a ferocious masculinity.

The Puerto Rican was living proof of the power of fashion, recently defamed in intellectual middle-class circles as a tool of hierarchy, a form of media control, or a symptom of superficiality. Fear of fashion is part of a new suspicion about surfaces and comes from the claim that beauty is inner and hidden and that the surfaces of our bodies are cynical fields of deception. Fashion, once a universal tool of originality, fantasy, and personal power—open to anyone with imagination and a capacity for sensuality and harmony—has suddenly become suspect. A new anti-aesthetic conformity has prevailed, cloaked in anodyne terms like "casual." Anyone who broaches this conformity is thought to have moral failings, for our bodies have been recast as indifferent packages containing inviolable souls.

I believe that people who speak contemptuously of fashion are superficial. Or as one of my friends, the deceased novelist Ursule Molinaro, said, "Why speak ill of the surface when only the void has none?" That fashion is surface is, of course, undeniable. But what exactly is surface? Fundamentally, it's the only data available to the human mind on a day-to-day basis. It follows, then, that a denial of surface, always espoused on moral grounds, is inevitably a denial of knowledge. Those who seek what they call a "deeper meaning" may actually be regressing into an imageless world of darkness, into a kind of unintentional narcissism.

Surface is the shining perimeter of our existence, just like the surface of the Earth upon which we live. Beneath it is formless, unintelligible matter. So how did surface get such a bad name? The answer to that question is complex because the denial of surface as the fount of meaning was an unintended collaboration between two supposedly opposed schools of thought: idealism and empiricism. Plato reduced surface and sensory images to shadows on the wall of a cave, a seductive spectacle for unenlightened fools. The empiricists dissected it into meaningless atoms, from which they composed a paint-by-number world. But like Aldous Huxley, I see surfaces as magical doors to perception, the canvases upon which the secrets of the soul appear as clearly as if written on a wall.

What creates the multitude of differences on the surface of the human body? Biology, genetics, yes, but also personal history. What magic art of horticulture grew the creases at the corners of this person's lips, the welling saucer eyes of that other, that one's upturned chin or hunched shoulders? Worry and childhood trauma, wonder at the behavior of others, entrenched pride, a sense of defeat. Why do satin skin and a face of classical proportions fill us with a sense of wonder, disbelief, desire or resentment? The visceral language of surface, which is beauty, touches us at the deepest levels of meaning.

"You're a 'lookist'!" shrieked a feminist friend as she watched me ogle prominent cheekbones, plush lips, and columnar necks in a men's fashion magazine. "I don't care how a man looks," she continued proudly. "I'm interested in his mind!" Did she think I was paging through a manual for embalmers? Why couldn't she understand that the surface of the living body is form animated by spirit, a crystal ball revealing human character?

In fact, the romantic ideal of love at first sight has a more realistic basis than most would claim. Written on the face, body, and gestures are more than half a person's inner life and entire past. All it takes to read them is a spectator who hasn't shut down his senses in the name of a so-called higher purpose. I've rarely met anyone who wasn't a near match in character to the way he or she looked. Getting to know that person better has merely filled in the categories. Which brings us back to fashion. Fashion is the surface that further articulates our very articulate surfaces. It's the more conscious appendage of the involuntarily communicating human form.

When you think about it, fashion may be the only universal, classless form of communication. Consider, in light of this, the urban poor, who have little more than their bodies to call their own. Note, for example, the high level of physical culture and action among the very poor, their proud, exaggerated strutting on the street. Such people possess only the clothing on their backs, however humble that wardrobe may be. Fashion, or dress, then, is an inalienable power, granted in some form to all but the naked. And in the United States, beginning in the late seventies, designers suddenly discovered who was setting some of the fashion trends. It wasn't the rich. The story is familiar now. First athletic suits, then banjee jewelry, then finally tattoos found their way into the lexicon of mainstream design. This is another power of the medium of fashion: at the very moment classes seem to be sequestered from one another, fashion steps forth, cynically or celebratively, to display bridges of identification among them.

In this new century, fashion has suddenly found itself facing a huge crisis. In the name of a fantasy, and only a fantasy, of a new classlessness, fashion has falsely positioned itself as the great leveler. The trend away from stylization in contemporary fashion is a false ideal with a hidden, predatory agenda. It's an attempt to convince the world that elitism is dead and that no one holds the power—for the very purpose of wielding that power more subtly. The drab world of the new casualness is a sinister threat, to the future not only of fashion but also of individuality, of creative expression and its resultant community among humankind.

In defiance of Georges Bataille, we've forgotten that the unconscious structure of all human groups is ritualistic, sexual, or sacred, and that ritual requires costume as well as pomp, etiquette, and other stylized structures. Covertly aided by puritanical ideals and a resurgence of the platonic, intellectuals are urging us toward antifashion as a way of escaping the Spectacle; they are convincing us of the need for the neutralization of surface signs, projecting distrust onto our senses and appearances. In the geometric-field uniforms of a sports player, the T-shirt and jeans of a manual laborer, or the summer shorts once reserved only for children, we're supposed to prove our liberality, our sense of equality, and our freedom from social control. But is this clothing any different from the dove-gray uniforms once worn by all the supporters of Mao? In our boastfully casual clothes, we now go about lives programmed for drabness, like stunted pilgrims in a Protestant community devoid of libidinal expression. Our alibi? That fashion was once a harmful way of distinguishing the rich from the poor. That merchandising is part of the delirious Spectacle designed to keep us enslaved.

I know that this is a mistake, simply because the visceral language of fashion has always been and is still the most flexible appendage of personal signification, transcending all language barriers. Whether we like it or not, fashion remains a way for the poor to invade the sight of the rich with inescapable, aggressive imagery. It is speech that can't be silenced.

When the Puerto Rican got off the subway, I got off, too, like a fish following the glimmer of a bright lure. I followed him closely, stopping when he did, to check his appearance in the reflection of a store window. Then we struck up a conversation, and I invited him to have a drink. A short discussion about money ensued, and when we got to my apartment, he removed each article of clothing. He folded the net T-shirt lovingly, to avoid causing any wrinkles. But as his pleated trousers fell away from his smooth, hard thighs, another level of surface was revealed: two enormous tattoos, portraying saints from the Catholic liturgy. Sex between us became a rite, full of iconic images and arcane gestures, which we watched in my bedside mirror. It was stylized but original, akin to the Latin root of fashion, *factio*, which means "the act of making."

In our current, sham utopias of imagined equality, how have we come to exile the multiple delights of adornment? Could it be that the leveled, denatured world of contemporary clothing is a disguise? Today, even the rich dress down, calling it discretion, attributing it to a new humility. But this new blandness resembles the cover effected by a double agent, wandering unchecked among the common people, concealing his vicious strategies for power and control.

America's
New Networkers

Blond, with a shirt that just happened to be unbuttoned low on the soft skin of his chest and pants that really should have been a size larger, the cute young songwriter gazed at me with tears in his wounded twenty-year-old doe eyes. Several copies of his handmade CDs were spread out on the table between us. Why, he wanted to know, was I being so mean? Hadn't he, after all, read an entire book by me, and hadn't he gone through the trouble of looking me up in the phonebook and ringing my doorbell to tell me how much he admired me as a writer? Then, because he just happened to have his work with him, he was hoping I'd be kind enough to listen to it and perhaps hook him up with a contact in the music world. After all, as a published writer, I must know a lot of interesting people.

Such a predictable outcome to our encounter had made me fly into a rage. I'd been polite enough when he rang the doorbell and interrupted my long soak in the tub, and I'd reacted with the requisite humility and pleasure as he heaped the kind of flattery upon me I'd heard from others his age numerous times before. But when he pulled out those CDs and went into the usual networking song and dance about "contacts," I suddenly became very hostile, enough to bring real tears to my sensitive and tender admirer's eyes.

This was a scene I'd repeated countless times in the new America, where all accomplishments among the young are rumored to be carried out with the help of the "powerful." A new networking virus has seized the youth of my country, traveling like wildfire through the brains of anyone hoping to accomplish something in the creative arts.

Certainly, I had no responsibility to grace his invasion of my privacy with any effort at education, but some compulsion to set the young man straight started me on a rant. I leaned across the table and gripped the now trembling shoulders, knowing that such a gesture would comprise the only physical contact we'd ever have.

I launched into a hysterical oration.

"Tell me, Larry [for that was the youth's name], which celebrities did Bob Dylan network with, flirt with, try to meet, or even fuck to get where he is today? The answer: none. Dylan comes from a time when narcissism, exhibitionism, and, oh yes, hard work and creativity, were still the only tools of the trade. The idea of 'meeting the right people,' expending some of your creative energy to set up a mini-self-promotion agency, wasn't on the front burner. Drive and talent did most all of it. Isn't that quaint, Larry? He actually thought his talent would carry him through!

"Bob and his sixties generation were the last to subscribe to the old myth of the creative genius. Unfortunately, I myself still operate by those stone-age methods. It may seem incredible today, but it was once considered beneath an artist to do his own marketing. The cranking out of flyers and invitations, the false patter of cocktail schmoozing, the gossipy jangle of telephones, or a mind for business were considered alien to the artist's creativity. Somebody else took care of that shit!

"Now, Larry, compare Bob Dylan to yourself, a twenty-year-old inexperienced musician who came east from Portland to make it in New York. For you, each day is a trade-off between developing what you think is your very original musical style and finding ways to get it noticed. It's obvious that you take it for granted that nobody will ever know your name unless you stick it in his face. And I'm sure you copped that hip Dior-model-inspired haircut for free from a friend in beauty school, learned to overcome your natural shyness so that you could crash parties, and practiced flipping the hair out of your face in the mirror so you can do it at the parties you crash. Next, you've put together a massive mailing list—on the computer your dad bought you—of people whose cards you've snatched at parties when they weren't feeling self-protective because they were high, then produced your own CD with ripped-off cover art, and tried to place it with a real record company by sucking up to the very people you once read about in seventh grade in fashion magazines and idolized but, now that you've met them, have already learned to detest.

"All this self-promotion is taking the bite out of your creativity, Larry. I'll bet that before you came to New York, you were knocking out a song a week. Now you've been pushing the same demo for over a year. But because of people like you, artists who are spending more time on their work will never get noticed. There's just too much aggressive marketing competition, and real artists don't have time.

"You may say, Larry, that you're acting out that time-old tale of an ingénue come to the big city. Learning the ropes. But if you yourself were to stop your incessant networking and check out some old movies, you'd see that ingénues from the sticks used to have all kinds of kinky, pleasurable adventures in New York. It wasn't all grim publicity work. Such isn't the case for you, Larry, because unlike the climbers of the past, you aren't even sticking your twenty-year-old dick into the holes of people with clout. No, little Larry, you wouldn't dream of dirtying your dick in any of the big names you've already managed to meet. Orgasms and all that other messy stuff would rob from the time you need for pure self-promotion. And as far as you're concerned, publicity is just as much a part of your work as a good bass line.

"Who do you fledging artists focus all your networking skills on, Larry, have you ever thought of that? Mostly established old farts around my age; though in my case you've made another naive error because I'm not established in the slightest. You baby networkers don't bother networking each other, just those who you think are on the rung above. Unfortunately, your judgment is not always the sharpest, and you unwittingly waste your precious time bothering small wheels like me. Tradition says that a young artist hits big time just in time to push the older ones into pasture. 'Hey, old man, get off the pot, it's time for our generation to take over.' But these days, new artists want favors before they give their former heroes the sole of their boot. 'Say, Dad, would you mind promoting my career, listening to my demo, and taking me by the hand to your agent before I push you off the roost so that I can become the next house-hold word?'

"The situation has created an interesting intergenerational dynamic. Aging artists who made it by sheer will are getting hustled by minor ace self-promoters who think it's written in heaven that they should be groomed. As I already pointed out, the casting couch is no longer part of the bargain. Forgive me for repeating this fact, but as somebody who had to suck his share of celebrity dicks, I just can't get over this change in the rules.

"According to the new ethos, all that's necessary is to ask for help relentlessly, or should I say, whine for it. This, however, doesn't rule out good cock-teasing skills. That's why you're wearing such a fetching outfit today, Larry. All you baby networkers are hip to the value of the seductive, sleazy come-on. If you've mastered any art to perfection, it's how to project flirtation without ever delivering. Perhaps starting at home with your parents, you learned how to turn older people on, or at least touch their hearts, stimulate their protective instincts, or make them feel guilty.

"By the way, Larry, my friend Bruce LaBruce, the film-maker, developed his 'Eve' theory a few years ago from the

Bette Davis movie *All About Eve*. It might interest you. Davis plays a Broadway actress on the verge of obsolescence who meets a supposedly adoring 'fan' named 'Eve.' Slowly but surely, she begins to take over Davis's life and career. So invaded was Bruce LaBruce's life by fledging boyish filmmakers after the success of his first two films that he began to use such sentences as 'He's an Eve' or 'Watch out, he'll Eve you.' It got so bad that he began seeing Eves in all people named St*eve* or flinched when a younger artist said 'Good *eve*ning.' His film sets became a kind of halfway house for flinty, brittle starlet boys, who did *eve*rything in their power to break his balls and always left him frustratingly blue-balled.

"Maybe the worst aspect of the baby networker phenomenon is the callousness with which you approach established talent. Not only don't you fuck stars, but—and this is really appalling—you show little interest in the older person's work. In the past, young, worshipful artists sought out culture heroes who'd inspired them. These groupies were the types who'd memorized every word or chord progression of their favorite celebrity. William Burroughs had a string of them. So did aging rock stars and stuffy old poets like James Merrill. Even that old Nazi sympathizer Leni Riefenstahl, who filmed for Hitler and lived to 101, still had a young buck-bottom to carry her camera equipment right up until the end. When these old-fashioned idolizers finally met their idols, they were always full of admiration and awe. They wished only to serve and learn.

"Not so today. Fledging artists like you don't worship idols, you merely fix them in your sights as potential targets. Imagine somebody working Shakespeare or James Joyce 'cause they knew he was well positioned in the 'industry.' There they'd sit, yawning during *Hamlet* or admitting that *Ulysses* put them to sleep while in the same gesture slapping some half-baked adolescent manuscript or a homemade CD down for him to read or listen to.

"As the writer of a cult novel about street life, this has happened to me on several occasions. For example, one afternoon a few years ago, a young, hot, flirtatious artist— from the provinces, like you; with a giant bulge in his rolled-up Calvin jeans, like yours; who was all dewy-eyed and in-sinuatingly complimentary, like you—was waiting at my doorstep when I got home from the proctologist. Foolish me let him in. From the beginning, there was something slightly blank and insolent about him that raised one of LaBruce's 'Eve' flags. But since I'd been programmed by an earlier gen-eration to respect groupies, and since he had a beautiful ass, I actually sat down with him and edited one of his short sto-ries for free. Then I gave him a free ticket to a big reading I was giving. How sweet it felt to have a worshipful protégé at my side as I strode into the lecture hall of the New York Pub-lic Library! I didn't know what I was in for. There's nothing more humiliating for an aging writer than watching the twenty-two-year-old he's just introduced to his agent skip-ping out of the room before he's even started reading. I never even got to jerk him off in the library john.

"Suzy Z is a twenty-one-year-old model who doesn't think her squeaky suburban-California voice is a hindrance to a crossover into acting. As a model, she learned to project convincingly all kinds of weary, heroin-chic, urban, working-class, whorish personae. To tell the truth, she was damned good at it. Not having spent much time sensitizing herself to her own or others' feelings, she sees acting as little more than a timed series of attitudes. I won't tell you whose personal assistant she's managed to become. The woman, in her late fifties, is one of our most respected living film actresses, but she's old enough, and I guess narcissistic enough and medicated enough, to believe that Suzy Z worships all her films. The truth is, Suzy only saw one of them on TV while she was doing speedballs with her out-of-work dot-com boyfriend. They fell asleep just after she gathered enough information to flatter her new boss. The legendary star-boss is too blurred out on pills to notice that Suzy doesn't know many facts. Meanwhile, Suzy has copied down all the names and numbers from the old bag's speed dial.

"How can someone of moderate talent be presumptuous enough to work a real, accomplished icon of the preceding generation? Perhaps the answer lies in the steamy, unhealthy relationships between you baby networkers and your baby boomer parents. Your permissive parents didn't create an atmosphere of authority or discipline to be rebelled against, like my parents did. That's where all my productivity comes from. The need to defy and escape my parents' authority made me strive for independence and self-reliance and kept me from an impulse for shameless sucking up. I had my own identity and was too proud to come begging to the older generation.

"On the other hand, it seems to be no accident that you new self-promoters come from a generation that often has trouble leaving the nest. Why struggle to get your own apartment when Dad doesn't mind you fucking your girlfriend at home? Why seek to make it on your own when Mom thinks you're the cat's pajamas just as you are? The situation seems to have created an intergenerational intimacy just ripe for feelings of entitlement on the part of the younger generation. In a way, networking and self-promotion are a lot like asking Daddy for the keys to the car. Because baby-boomer parents spent too much time 'fraternizing' with their children and let them act out all kinds of family romance scenarios at home, the new generation are like pampered whores who believe that the previous generation owes them a living and should be shamelessly cajoled into doing favors.

"The idea of the artist as a package is a relatively recent one. Even Mick Jagger didn't start out with much more than a guitar, a haircut, a voice, and some junkies-to-be as backup. At the beginning, when he created his most memorable music, he was no mediatized Marilyn Manson. Neither was Bob Dylan, of course. Probably the first person in rock to veer from art and self-reliance into a corporate-inspired kind of packaging was David Bowie, whose glam revolution turned rock—a fairly straightforward working-class cultural phenomenon—into an upwardly mobile effort obsessed with social hobnobbing and glamour. Bowie's art was still good music, but it was also an ingenious new business enterprise that involved hundreds of opportunistic people and glittering ambitions. Clothing, lighting, hairdos, and other eye-catching publicity techniques began to become more important than the music.

"That's one reason why we'll play old Jagger more than we'll play old Bowie fifty years from now. The new culture of self-promotion has had a disastrous effect upon creation.

Networked art has the shelf life of a tomato. Energy spent networking is the same energy that could be spent making potential masterpieces. Listen, you can spend your creativity on your art or spend it on conning the world into noticing you. Either way, you use it up. It's up to you to decide how.

"Check out recent history, and you'll realize that the early fame that results from self-promotion doesn't seem to make anything but flashes in the pan. There's nothing worse, I think, than being acknowledged too early. Often, it can discourage you from struggling onward. If we want to get deeper about this, we might say new networkers like you lacked creative impetus in the first place. You try to cover up this lack with self-publicity. It hides the black hole of emptiness in your psyche. Again, this might come from your relationship with your parents. Rage against parents was tangible with the older generations and thus more available as creative material. Rebellion creates a distinct identity. Young people today like you also hate their parents, but it's a buried, passive-aggressive anger. You can't really pin anything on your permissive Mom and Dad, but in some repressed way, you'd like to disembowel them. In your case, rage exists more in denial. It's less accessible to creativity. What I'm trying to say is that you lack material.

"Time will tell what will happen when you become the older generation, Larry. From the way things are going, you can't be expected to be listened to or read by the generation below you. But maybe this is appropriate, since your output will be mostly composed of publicity. The young who try to exploit you won't find anything but waning influence, power, and marketing strategies. Yet you'll probably try to charge them for that, too."

By the time I got to the end of my lecture, I noticed a strange but to-be-expected phenomenon. My young guest, Larry, who'd flinched as if horribly wounded at the beginning of my speech, had slowly lapsed into a state of nonreaction. He wasn't looking at me now but seemed to be staring at something else in the room. It was then that I remembered another characteristic of the new American generation: attention deficit disorder. Still, he sat there quite respectfully, like any well-brought-up youth who has been taught by his parents not to interrupt adults when they're speaking. Then, seeing that I'd finally finished my monologue, he turned his attention to me again and revealed what he'd been considering.

"Is that a good ink-jet printer you have?" he asked politely. "Think I could use it to print a couple covers for my CD? All I got is a cheap printer, and the ones I made will never grab attention."

2

Men in My Life

Tel Quel's
Gaudy Harlequin

Paris is a city of gray subtleties, but in 1973 it was shattered momentarily by a grimacing, burly Cuban named Severo Sarduy, scrambling across the street in low-cost, bright-orange, striped bell bottoms. A car swerved and honked angrily as Sarduy struck a Kabuki pose of effeminate fright. When he reached the opposite side, his young and brilliant American translator, Suzanne Jill Levine, introduced him to me. His hand felt thick. He was raucous and manic, with campy gestures that outranked Carmen Miranda's. This was the revered Cuban member of the prestigious post-structuralist Tel Quel literary group—the intellectual partner of Roland Barthes and Jacques Lacan.

The Parisian contradiction of Severo Sarduy deepened for me in 1975, after Suzanne Jill Levine handed me her translation of his novel *Cobra*. As if with a machete, I hacked my way through a text I can only describe as "tropical"—overfoliated, procreative, and intricate. But by tropical I also mean ever-vigilant, unblinking like the sun; for, to keep from going mad from the heat, tropical writing is always rigorously structured. Behind the riot of Sarduy's fiestas are months of grueling rehearsal. Severo Sarduy was a baroque comedian and a callused workhorse in one.

Rigorous discipline imposed upon steaming chaos is what most endeared this hyperactive Carmen Miranda act-alike to the Tel Quel crowd. His novel *Cobra,* which was rendered into French with the help of Philippe Sollers, can be called narrative—if the reader can accept every one of its atomic sentences as a narrative complete and self-enclosed. Each jewel-like sentence is structured with tawdry detail, only to unfold like an origami trick into a new and more convoluted gesticulation, a new sacrilege. Behold:

> The queen had hung herself, from the ceiling, by her feet, an upside-down hanging: slave chains hung her by the ankles to the base of a lamp. She was an albino bat among opalescent glass balloons and quartz chalices. Forming meanders, her hair fell among ceramic reeds, scorching themselves on the transparent gladioluses of the lampshades. The clinking of the hanging fruit was that of a Japanese mobile at the entrance of a monastery in flames.

Within the fidgety gymnastics of *Cobra* is a story thread. A transvestite named Cobra, who performs in the Lyrical Theater of Dolls, is obsessed with shrinking her feet to a more feminine size. Her assistants, Madam and Pup, who is

the dwarf double of Cobra, also change shape. This meta-
morphosis occurs during a motorcycle gang-bang initiation,
which changes everybody into Tibetan lamas on a flat, rather
fake Tibetan landscape.

Tortured plot notwithstanding, getting there is all the
fun. My friendship with Levine and my later attempt to
translate a short piece of Sarduy's written in French were
to teach me that the best way to read Sarduy—outside the
academy—is to translate him. Critics have made much of
his cultural displacements, the eruptions of his native Cuba
by many migrations followed by his own transplantation to
Paris. On this losing ground, he shifts signification by means
of diabolical puns and specious referents, moving from high-
class post-structuralist terminology to pop culture, from the
language of physics to queer argot, or from tacky touristic remarks to flashes of Buddhist transcendence.

Sarduy is the quintessential sixties writer, irreverent, vo-
racious, parodic, with a taste for Zen. He's like a New Age
devotee on mescaline expounding on the Tarot. Something's
wrong with the scholarship, but he knows it. He's a polymorphous Angel of Light doing an imitation of Bette Davis
talking about "the Chinese quarter" in the film *The Letter.*
Sarduy's glittering, mutating images—which signify everything with great fanfare, but finally signify nothing—are
built on a void. It's kind of like an acid trip.

Another novel, *Maitreya,* opens in Tibet at the moment of
the Chinese invasion, then journeys to Cuba in preparation
for revolution, where we meet the reborn Buddha, known as
Maitreya, who will be reincarnated in the person of Cuban
Chinese cook Luis Leng. Again, the author's images are as

garishly decked out as a Miami Beach dowager. And again, mutation is drastic and dizzying. But this time the prose has a painterly lyricism that sometimes borders on the sedate. *Maitreya* is one of the most beautiful and radiant texts I have ever read, as seamless as a single ocean wave, spilling us from high elegance to low camp and back again without pausing.

> Lady Tremendous lay sprawling as if she'd been poured from above: a pink soufflé. On the floor a bold volunteer—wearing contact lenses and a nurse's uniform—with flesh-pot's face between her legs as if giving birth to her, sans douleur, buried her heels in the carpet as she pulled on Co-lossal's black garters: the stockings rose like a glove around the rolls of pulp, dilated like a boa devouring a lamb.

No critic has discussed Sarduy's work without heavy reference to the metaphor of transvestitism. His linguistic transformations purposely play on the idea of culture as a transvestizing process. Identity has no real core. Like the cosmetic rituals Sarduy often describes—and perhaps like Cuba itself—history is a slapdash slathering on of ethnic and historical layers. Colonization is a sloppy wardrobe mistress yanking wigs and corsets onto breathless vaudevillians. Language, in which word rakishly overlays meaning, is a tacky transvestizing medium as well.

Nowhere is this metaphor more evident than in Sarduy's 1967 novel *From Cuba with a Song*. This send-up of Cuban history is divided into three parts, devoted to three major ethnic elements of Cuba: Chinese, African, and Spanish. It ends with the coming of Christ. Or is it Castro's arrival in Havana?

The transvestites in *From Cuba with a Song* are "meta-transvestites" for they can change not only from men into women but from queens into leather-clad American bikers. Change is easy in all of Sarduy's work, because nothing is real—or even convincing. In a preface to the current American edition of *Cobra* and *Maitreya,* Suzanne Jill Levine makes it clear that for Sarduy, South Asian culture could never be more than "costume jewelry India." "I believe," he said, "that the only decoding a Westerner can do, that the only unneurotic reading that is possible from our logocentric point of view, is that which India's surface offers. The rest is Christianizing translation, syncretism, real superficiality."

Beneath this opting for the surface is, of course, a certain kind of intellectual striving that flees superficiality and seeks meaning. Abstruse reading and writing occupied Sarduy right up to his death from AIDS in 1993. The master of frivolity was a serious artist. The sputtering Catherine wheels of his writing are the result of the crushing machinery of his intellect, something that put him in league with the Parisian gray-hair-splitters of post-structuralism, that linked him to their painstaking scholarship and teeth-gnashing erudition. However, his dizzy ostentation and hysterical playfulness stands out among them, like a bright hibiscus among the meticulously fitted slabs of gray marble.

The Spider Woman's
Mother

The name Manuel Puig, often pronounced "Pooj" in Mexico, isn't overly familiar in my Anglo-Saxon literary world, but in Latin America, at least in literary circles, it rivals that of the great Argentine linguistic master Jorge Luis Borges, also from Argentina. Fifteen years after his death in 1990, Puig remains for every Latin American intellectual a part of a pantheon of writers, among whom are names more familiar to American writers, such as Gabriel García Márquez (Colombia), and names less familiar to some of us in America, such as Guillermo Cabrera Infante, Severo Sarduy, and Reinaldo Arenas (Cuba); Julio Cortázar, Silvina Ocampo, and Bioy Casares (Argentina); Pablo Neruda and Isabel Allende (Chile); Jorge Amado (Brazil); Carlos Fuentes (Mexico); and Mario Vargas Llosa (Peru). Despite this,

Manuel Puig's career, as well as his emotional life, was intimately connected to the American scene, as evidenced by his greatest triumph in this country, the novel *Kiss of the Spider Woman,* which was adapted into an Academy Award–winning movie in 1985 and later into a successful Broadway musical directed by Hal Prince. My close and rewarding friendship with Manuel, which began when we met in 1974 and lasted until his death sixteen years later, remains remarkable to me because of the quixotic nature of his personality. It taught me how inadequate most social judgments and first impressions are and confirmed the principle that the most gifted and creative people—geniuses, in fact—are sometimes hiding under the most unlikely exteriors.

In the mid-1970s, when Manuel Puig was asked to contribute to a book of self-portrait drawings by writers, he sent in a simple line drawing of a mouse. It was an accurate metaphor of his social persona. Slightly stooped, with thinning hair and a once-handsome face, wearing drab clothing, he gave the impression of a milquetoast bank clerk, an effeminate homosexual mama's boy with a shuffling step and a bathetic, bemused smile. In English, his Spanish accent and his whiny intonation seemed comical. He was, in addition, according to most people's evaluation, a film buff of the lowest caste, one among those legions of retiring obsessives who gorge themselves on mostly Hollywood films considered frivolous by serious intellectuals. Manuel was a walking encyclopedia of film trivia, carrying in his brain endless lists of acting credits—especially female—costume designers, and titles. This obsession arose from a dreary 1930s and 1940s childhood in a small town on the Argentine pampas, which he'd spent mostly at movie matinees with a fantasizing mother, both of them escaping from an ill-tempered and dictatorial father and husband, into a lavish and synthetic world of celluloid, hackneyed romantic gestures, and glamorous gowns. Manuel's entire childhood and adolescence had been devoured by overweening fantasies inspired by these films, hours and hours spent pretending that he, too, would one day live the ecstasies of a Greta Garbo, a Joan Crawford, or a Jean Harlow.

How this seemingly trivial mania became the basis for some of the most intricate literary constructions and penetrating cultural analyses of the second half of the twentieth century, in the novels *Betrayed by Rita Hayworth, Heartbreak Tango, Pubis Angelical, Blood of Requited Love, Kiss of the Spider Woman, The Buenos Aires Affair, Eternal Curse of the Reader of These Pages,* and *Tropical Night Falling*—the eight books that represent his entire novelistic output—is a question for alchemists. However, during my first year of friendship with Manuel, when he was already a highly acclaimed writer, he tried to answer the question in his own inimitably humble manner at a scholarly conference on Latin American literature at New York University. "My life on the pampas," he explained in his mewling tones, "was a B movie. So I did a remake of it in these novels, reaching for the A rating."

Manuel's project was, in reality, a much subtler and more complex one. In each of these eight novels, using new techniques of narrative that looked deceptively simple on the surface, he set up an amazing dialectic between our inner worlds of fear, yearning, desire, and sexuality and the synthetic, commoditized world of our culture. His miracle is the lack of bias and the respect he accorded each half of the dichotomy. Interweaving the clichés of Hollywood into situations, dialogues, dreams, and even politics, he not only revealed their absolute penetration into virtually every aspect of our consciousness but also elevated cultural clichés to true archetypal status, on the same level as Greek myth. Finally, the process he invented also salvaged his own life from triviality. By some form of magic, he managed to prove that the stereotypical pop feminine ideals that had contaminated his life were actually sublime models of human struggle.

Most of Manuel Puig's novels were published here in the 1970s and early 1980s, when the publisher Dutton was struggling to find a market for the new wave of Latin American literature. *Kiss of the Spider Woman,* his third novel, which was banned in Argentina at the time of its Spanish-language release in 1976, takes place in that totalitarian country. Told wholly in dialogue, like an overblown playscript that would take more than a full day if it were actually performed, it tells the story of two prison inmates, thrown together by a repressive regime with the aim of increasing their humiliation. One, a Marxist revolutionary, has been arrested for violent activism striving to liberate the oppressed common people of Argentina. The other, an effeminate homosexual arrested for a sex crime, represents, ironically, those very common people the Marxist is supposedly struggling for. Over a series of nights in degraded surroundings—punctuated by the sound of torture; devoid of nourishing food, much light, and other sources of stimulation—the homosexual assumes a Scheherazade-like role, recounting in detail the plots of his favorite movies, insinuating them into the space between the two, like a spider weaving a web. The revolutionary, who considers himself too serious for these degrading narratives drawn from capitalist confections, is repulsed at first. But the film buff's visceral immersion in the hackneyed plots begins to overwhelm him, and their imaginative content becomes more and more subversive, that is to say, revolutionary. Gradually, the two characters mutate, assuming each other's roles. The disturbing power of the human imagination is revealed as a genuine tool of cultural revolution. The revolutionary's values are revealed to be clichéd. The petty fantasies of the homosexual film buff expand into universal truths, and his physical attraction for the revolutionary becomes a kind of salvation. An intellectual and emotive process of agape takes place, and both men transcend their own self-involvement.

In *Blood of Requited Love,* a novel published in 1982, Manuel opted for a wholly other examination of cultural cliché and visited another form of mental incarceration. This time he entered the brain of a Brazilian macho, a failed and frustrated would-be soccer player whose unending dialogue with his own poor self-esteem plunges deeper and deeper into creative fantasy. This novel is distinguished by its quirky form: it's composed entirely of an interview occurring inside the soccer player's head but uses only the third person. For example, a voice will ask, "Where did he meet her?" Another voice inside the soccer player's mind will answer for him: "He met her . . ."

I met Manuel Puig through a prolific translator of Latin American literature, Suzanne Jill Levine. By that point already, Manuel's life wasn't easy. Because of the fascistic political climate in his country, he was persona non grata and lived as an exile in New York for several years. This was painful for him primarily because of his passionate attachment to his mother, whom he saw only when he could bring her to New York or travel with her to the many exotic countries around the world where his books were being published. He was also growing older and finding that the sexual and romantic escapades that had inspired him and blotted out his loneliness in the past were getting fewer and farther between. More than ever, he had need of the fantasy world of his childhood, in which Hollywood scenarios of passion, glamour, and fulfillment blotted out life's shabby disappointments.

Puig's rich, ambiguous narratives resulted from his total commitment to fantasy and his ability as a thinker and creator to transform these fantasies into viable and penetrating analyses of culture, but not everyone knew that he tried to perform the same magic on the experiences of daily life. Such play-acting, in which he would assume numerous female personae and transform the identities of his close friends by a similar process, often drew scornful laughter or disbelief from the people he encountered. However, in reality, his life was an object lesson for all of us who are sure we know the difference between the trivial and the relevant. On the surface, he seemed to be a ridiculous, nearly half-mad, superficial person, drifting sighingly into vapid fantasies inspired by Garbo or Hedy Lamarr, the actress upon whom his novel *Pubis Angelical* is based. In fact, he imitated Garbo with such accuracy that today I can't watch her films without seeing him. When I do, it seems as if it is she who is doing an imitation of Manuel. Underneath this parodic surface, however, was an individual of deep ambition and ingenuity, a linguistic genius, an extremely calculating businessman and a shrewd observer of the human soul. He was the most effeminate man I've ever met, but his pretensions of being a woman, which he often comically claimed to be, were really evocations of the cultural nature of all sex roles. Manuel's woman was a cultural construction, and it defied us to find any evidence for gender beyond this category.

Just as he did in his books, Manuel mythologized and streamlined his social interactions, ritualistically studding them with hilarious nicknames and feminine patter. He spoke only in the feminine gender, which must have sounded even more surreal in gender-inflected Spanish but which could lead to some hysterically funny gender malapropisms in English. All of his closest friends who were younger than him were referred to as his "daughters," and he baptized each of them with a feminine moniker. My somewhat wild and experimental searches for pleasure and the late hours I kept inspired him to compare me to a young girl of the Jazz Age, and henceforth I was always referred to as "la Flapper" or "la môme." Another younger friend around my age was more retiring and also more obedient when Manuel requested favors. He dubbed this friend, whose last name was Mandelbaum, "La Mandelbaum," and maintained that he was a regular "Floradora girl," referring to the youthful female standard of beauty near the turn of the century in America. "La môme," he'd moan to me, "why can't you be like your sister, La Mandelbaum. Now there's a real Floradora girl." He took this language to such extremes that our conversations were perpetually bathed in it. A couple of years after Watergate, when the impeachment of Nixon was being discussed on television, Manuel uttered a "tsk, tsk," and said, "Oh, la Nixon, what a bad girl, such a mess she created with la Vietnam."

Manuel's daring and ridiculous distortions of linguistic social norms weren't just tics. They were expressions of a lithe flexibility of persona and a lack of moral judgments about others. During a week he spent in my apartment while visiting New York from Rio, I was in the midst of getting legal custody of a homeless Puerto Rican boy of fourteen, whom I'd taken pity on in the streets of Times Square. At the same time, I was also working full-time as the assistant to Robert Craft, the former secretary of Igor Stravinsky and the inheritor of his estate. Not having placed my charge in any school yet, I had to leave him home when I went to work. Because this boy was staying with me, I'd found Manuel one-week lodgings in a friend's apartment across the hall from mine. Unbeknownst to me, my charge was having wild drug and sex parties with several of his adolescent girlfriends while I was away working. One day I came home early and surprised them. I flew into a rage. But my charge interrupted my angry lecture by saying, "Well, Abuela didn't mind." Abuela means "granny" in Spanish. It turned out that he was referring to Manuel, who'd come into my apartment to catch a movie on television and had sat unperturbed amidst the wild partiers, telling all the Puerto Rican teenagers present to call him "abuela," or "granny," a moniker that seemed totally acceptable to them. That same year my charge and I sat watching the Academy Awards, and he was filled with pride when Abuela's film, *Kiss of the Spider Woman*, won an award for best actor.

Manuel's fantasy life fueled not only his books but also his increasingly lonely personal life. However, this got more difficult as the years went on. He'd moved to Rio and got his mother a house right next to his. Each of his days was regimented. He'd wake early, write immediately, and then go to his mother's for lunch. Then he'd return to his house and write some more. Then he'd go swimming for his health. Late afternoons three days a week usually entailed a "date" with one or another of the working-class men—all heterosexual—who'd become his hired paramours—the gardener, the janitor, or the neighborhood mechanic. True to form, he never questioned the family life of these contacts, and aside from paying them for their services, offered gifts to them, their wives, and their families. They all respected him. After one of these dates, he'd shower and return to Mama's for dinner.

Manuel's life would change in the late 1970s, after the invention of the VCR, which allowed him to quickly build up a massive cinema library. An evening film with Mama on video soon became part of Manuel's daily routine. Things were almost as they'd been when he was a child in General Villegas, when the two had gone to the movies together every single weekend. It was during this period that I was drafted into the gargantuan project of creating the world's largest personal video collection for Manuel and his mother. Or as Manuel put it, "You are now my video slave!" With two VCRs he bought on a trip up from Rio de Janeiro, I found myself spending nights and weekends copying tapes that were temporarily loaned from the most widespread sources, including secret contacts at the Museum of Modern

Art, the cinematographer Nestor Almendros, and Robert Gottleib, who was then editor in chief of *The New Yorker.*

By the late eighties, Manuel Puig's literary stature had become global. The success of *Kiss of the Spider Woman* as a film and a workshop production of the story bound for Broadway had made him a sought-after figure. He was still living in Rio at the time, but he came to New York for the out-of-town premiere of the musical, and we went to see it in a limousine provided by renowned Broadway director Hal Prince, during which Manuel moaned about the stage production being a massacre of his work.

In fact, each time Manuel came to New York, he would refuse the lavish hotel accommodations he was offered in favor of staying with me—his "daughter." As we watched one or another obscure silent or 1930s film on one of the VCRs, my phone would inevitably ring, and Manuel would beg me to play watchdog. At the time, Jane Fonda was considering producing and acting in a script he'd written; Madonna was interested in another that was based on the 1940s exotic Latin singer Yma Sumac, who was rumored in reality to be a Jewish girl from Brooklyn, Amy Camus, which is Yma Sumac spelled backwards; and the fashion designer Diane von Furstenberg wanted to go into publishing and buy several manuscripts from him. I found myself in the position of having to get rid of these media stars on the phone, because Manuel was too immersed in the melodrama playing on the VCR.

Manuel was generous to those whom he considered close friends, and he gave me some of my first literary opportunities. It was he who introduced me to French actor Jean-Pierre Aumont, which led to my first translation from the French, Aumont's memoirs. Manuel and I collaborated on a Mexican film fantasy about Marilyn Monroe for Rafael Corkidi, the cinematographer of the legendary Mexican film *El Topo*. I worked on the English version of a film about Rio that Manuel had written. He also tried, albeit unsuccessfully, to hook me up with the Hollywood machine after the success of *Kiss of the Spider Woman*. His narrative techniques have had a strong influence on my writing, and I still reread some of his books today.

In 1990, two weeks after his last visit to me in New York, and shortly after moving to Mexico into a lavish house he'd built for himself and his very ancient mother, Manuel was rushed to the hospital with a burst gallbladder. The operation seemed to be a success, but a day later he died of heart failure, during recovery, at the age of fifty-seven. There was a certain irony to his early demise: for years he'd shared his fear about his inability to go on after the death of his beloved mother, who was then in her eighties. It had never occurred to him that he could die before her. For years afterward, Manuel's mother lived an extremely comfortable life in Argentina on the proceeds of Manuel's many literary successes, managing his estate with his older brother.

Manuel seems to have left behind, however, one more irreverent joke about the culture of gender. A day or two after his death, an obituary appeared in the *New York Times*. The article said that he was survived by two sons, who lived in Mexico. It seems that his two favorite Mexican "daughters," who were really two middle-aged gay men about thirteen years his junior, had claimed this familial kinship out of a twisted sense of sentimentality and loyalty to his memory. Trying to set the record straight, I called the *New York Times.* They wouldn't believe me, and Manuel went down in history as the devoted father of two grown sons.

MANUEL PUIG
BORN: December 28, 1932, General Villegas, Argentina
DIED: July 22, 1990, Cuernavaca, Mexico

Montmartre's
Blue Angel

Eight floors above a small gated street in Montmartre reigns nightclub entrepreneur Michou, the French Liberace, perpetually sporting a blindingly azure blazer and Jackie O.–style blue-tinted glasses.

For more than thirty-five years, Michou's claim to fame has been a tiny club at 80 rue des Martyrs, called Chez Michou, which offers decent Picardian cuisine as well as a much loved Montmartre drag show. In this cramped cartoon paradise, whose red walls are hung with extravagantly gilded mirrors, performers reject the literal exactness of American female impersonation in favor of Molière-style caricature. Their exaggerated send-ups of Edith Piaf, Josephine Baker, Madonna, or Liza Minnelli hearken back to a time when royalty could be parodied but never directly criticized, on pain of death.

Both old Hollywood and old European "royalty," from Lauren Bacall to Mireille Mathieu, have made the pilgrimage up the steep Montmartre hillside to the little club to face their images in the distorted mirror of the minuscule stage and pay homage to their beloved Michou. Little did I think that such a touted French institution would prove to be such an egotistical diva. But, alas, what started innocently on the part of an American magazine called *nest* as an attempt to reveal to fans Michou's extravagant apartment became a struggle of wits between the willfully perverse club owner and their hired paparazzi.

It all began peacefully one morning in May 1998 at 10 a.m., as the darling of *tout Montmartre* was throwing on his pressed white pants and signature blue blazer. I was waiting with my reporter's pad and disposable camera at the entranceway, which is boastfully decorated with all the gold 45s Michou recorded long ago. His canvas-crowded foyer, into which I was next ushered, is more than he lets on. "Those paintings? They are just 'Monmartrois' [paintings by neighborhood artists]," he scoffed, as he yanked me away toward the living room. However, as I craned my neck backward, methinks I spied some genuine major and minor masters, such as Picasso, Lorjou, and Gen-Paul.

The "Blue Angel" of Montmartre had ostentatiously installed himself on his overstuffed couch upholstered in a blue and white flower pattern to match his blue and white costume, and I took the opportunity to snap a picture.

Responding with an ear-to-ear Carol Channing smile that drew attention to his stiff blond coiffure, he froze graciously, then grabbed a royal-blue cellular phone and began punching numbers into it, giving me a total of three minutes to dash about the house taking more snapshots.

As Michou's close friend Jean-Claude Baker, the adopted son of Josephine Baker and the author of her biography, explained, "Michou has no taste, which becomes, with him, great taste." And indeed, the quarters of this impresario, upon whom the queeny character Albin in the award-winning *La Cage aux Folles* was partly based, proved to be a place where the real melds shamelessly with the fake or where tasteless excess becomes high art through brazen bravado. From his dining room's faux Louis XV chairs to the pseudo-Bohemian chandelier; from the replicas of neoclassical busts and old masters to the real late Modernist canvases, what Michou could glean from French high culture as well as his fantasies about it have been used to fabricate a very kitsch though comically endearing environment. Like the actors at his club, Michou's apartment impersonates everything it's not, creating a transvestized illusion of wealth, culture, and elegance for those who were raised on pop.

The love child of a factory worker in Amiens, Michou fled to Paris in the early 1950s, while still an adolescent, to escape the dreary clothing factories in which he himself was already working. He landed in postwar Pigalle, which was then a fiefdom of Paris, replete with sex workers, mafiosos, and underhanded politicians. Photographs and the reports of friends who knew Michou at the time verify that his svelte physique and classical features, as well as his verve and directness, served him well on the rough streets. "He was the darling of Pigalle," says Baker, "a *titi* par excellence. This illiterate boy had come from the north to conquer the capital, and men and women of all ages were fighting to caress his gorgeous body." According to Baker, Michou often obliged, but with an eye toward entering just the right circles, some of which had connections to very right-wing politics.

Almost back to this period dates one of Michou's first collectibles, a small porcelain chocolate pot that used to stand among more recent treasures in his empire-style vitrine. "When Michou gives away the secret of how he acquired that pot," says Baker, "he will finally be at peace with himself."

Michou's craze for acquiring knock-offs, rather than originals, has continued even into the period of considerable wealth he now ostentatiously enjoys. Although he himself seems strangely unaware of the phenomenon, Jean-Claude Baker cautions: "Do you dare to call it a replica, if the person doesn't know the original? Who are you to tell him it's a fake when he arrived penniless in the streets of Paris and saw through the window of a shop in Pigalle—let's say a hairdresser's for pimps and prostitutes—a darling little chair, which he dreamed of owning some day! Our Michou did not begin his years looking through shop windows on the Champs-Elysées or St. Germain-des-Prés, thank you very much!"

Thus, the boy who once had nothing has spent his star-studded life cultivating a home that is in some ways a stylized caricature of old Montmartre high life, replete with its bohemian artists and cabaret flair for exaggeration. The same shades of differently patterned blue and white wallpaper stagily dominate all his rooms. In the dining room—as in the style of certain dining rooms in suburban America—the curtains are an extension of the pattern established by the wallpaper. Throughout this room is a profusion of blue glass or china bric-a-brac, including a large blue blown-glass bowl, adorned in a gold Modernist scrawl with Michou's name. There are also a gilt-framed fireplace (does it work? and if so, will the gold paint catch fire?) and windows with views of the terrace and the picturesque Butte.

During Michou's brief hours of rest away from the club—say, from 5 to 9 a.m.—he nestles in his quilted-walled bedroom of a rather feminine elegance, where the bed is flanked by two blue faux-marble rectangular night tables, holding gnarled gold chinoiserie lamps with little blue silk shades. Above this bed is a (probably fake) pompier—a formula painting, often of an erotic nature, done by certain minor artists of the late nineteenth century.

When Michou bathes (though whether or not alone these days also remains unknown), it is beneath a mirror etched with an art deco–style silhouette of Piaf, in a spacious fiberglass tub with a Jacuzzi, surrounded by bath salts in containers that are, of course, blue. Mirrored closets flank the hallway leading from the bed and bath to the rest of the apartment, so Michou never appears with a hair out of place.

My three minutes were up! Michou imperially waved off my questions about his life and his décor, merely punching more numbers into the blue phone and barking to his assistant to get together a packet of articles for me about his "past." (You can be sure that all of them were shallow and complimentary.) He climaxed my whirlwind visit by suggesting I take a snapshot of him on his terrace, on which he respread the Carol Channing smile against the campy background of the Sacré-Coeur.

Two months later, our professional photographer called Michou on his cellular to arrange taking genuine high-quality photos of his apartment. "I am at the hairdresser's!" barked Michou and promptly hung up. There followed a series of calls and faxes to His Highness of Camp reminding him of his promise to have his apartment photographed by us. Michou fielded all of them with rather transparent strategies: call me later; arrange it with the office; who are you; I don't remember you, etc. Brazen self-interest was finally revealed when one of his stooges sent us a fax explaining that Michou saw no immediate publicity gain for the club in bothering to let his apartment be photographed. I mean, who were we, anyway? Underneath this snobbery, I suspect, were some anxieties about thieves seeing the treasures sequestered in Michou's lair. He had been robbed in the past. And this was the reason he had downplayed his painting collection for me.

Undaunted by his refusals, we persisted by fax and phone, but in frustration my editor finally hired a brave surveillance photographer, who, night after night, scaled the scaffolding of a neighboring building, trying to peep into Michou's window. However, the wily impresario never seemed to be home, unless he was creeping around in the dark with the express purpose of foiling us. It's something I wouldn't put past him. Surely his flighty head did not remember, however, the snapshots that I'd hurriedly taken on that first day with my disposable camera. Having no other recourse, we presented them in *nest*.

Michou may consider himself a French icon, too exclusive or too specialized for the pages of an American magazine. But is he, like us, aware that his lavish apartment is a wry though unintended comment on the sanctity of French culture—both an accommodation of it and a riotous nose-thumbing at its weighty authority in interior design and architecture?

Jean-Claude Baker expects there will be a statue of Michou erected in the streets of Montmartre after his death. One hopes it will be of the finest quality marble. But, undoubtedly, it will lead to miniature knock-offs—in plaster of paris or blue plastic—which are certain to find their way perpetually to the mantelpieces of the Michous of the future.

A Champion
in Times Square

When we met in the late eighties, Emile Griffith, the legendary American boxer, was still a fixture in one or another of the hole-in-the-wall bars in Times Square's West 40s, with their eclectic mix of tourists, prostitutes, and guys from the 'hood. Perched on a bar stool and drinking Cuba Libres, he'd grin into the dark-circled eyes of homeboys wandering in from their all-day limbo in front of Port Authority, doling them out free drinks, dollar bills, or curses. You needed only to shake his hand to think twice about getting on the wrong side of him. Tapered and stiff as the paw of a marsupial, it was unbelievably callused and weighted with extra cartilage. Many people who came to these hangouts had no idea who they were dealing with, even when his first name would spill from his mouth with a strong Caribbean lilt. But once you realized whose hand you'd touched, if you knew anything at all about boxing, a shiver traveled down your spine. This was Emile Griffith, the sixty-something-year-old Virgin Islands immigrant and former six-time world champion in three weight divisions; and at Madison Square Garden on March 24, 1962, the hand grasping yours had delivered, on television, those lethal blows that pinned Benny "Kid" Paret against the ropes and led to his death at Roosevelt Hospital ten days later. It was a landmark event in the world of boxing and American television, later described by a shattered Norman Mailer, who'd seen it at close hand; and it led to an unsuccessful call among certain politicians to ban boxing as well as a reluctance on the part of the major TV networks to televise the sport again.

In 1997, three days before the thirty-fifth anniversary of his fatal fight with Paret, I sat with Griffith as he drank at a 47th Street club owned by Kathy Hogan. Kathy is an old-timer from Hell's Kitchen who—for a while—would survive the Times Square renovation by upscaling her establishment. As Hogan directed some workers who were moving the entrance to her club to make room for another tenant, who was building a celebrity hangout above her, Griffith reminisced about wandering the neighborhood in the wee hours on the night of the fight that had led to Paret's death. He'd gone to Roosevelt Hospital in hopes of apologizing to Paret and his family but was turned away. Some claimed that his fury in the ring was a direct result of what happened at the weigh-in, when Paret hurled at him a Cuban slang word meaning "faggot."

"I left that hospital and wandered along 42nd Street," Griffith told me. "'Cause that's where I always came to find my friends. But this time, a bunch of crazy shits who'd heard what happened were calling me some very ugly names."

The very first time Griffith walked through the streets of Times Square was in 1957, at the age of eighteen, on the way to deliver a package from the ladies hat company in the garment district where he worked. He rushed quickly past the gaming parlor Fascination, the dance halls, and the cheap movie theaters, without even looking up at the oversized billboards and neon lights. His boss, Howard Albert, who would later become his comanager, didn't want him to dawdle. Albert kept a close watch on Griffith, hustling the budding fighter to a boxing gym at 28th and 9th almost every day after work, then to one of the five Tad's Steakhouses in Times Square after training. Back then, if the pictures I later saw at Emile's were any evidence, he was a gorgeous sight to behold. Lean, ebony-skinned, and densely muscled, he had a flashing, white-toothed smile that was disturbingly disarming. There was a strange openness and vulnerability to that smile, which was probably connected to being a mama's boy. Griffith worshipped his Caribbean mother, and even in the cutthroat world of Times Square's seamy clubs, he was always looking for some maternal figure. Kathy Hogan, for example, had played that role for years, bundling a drunken Griffith into a taxi when he drank too much, locking up his valuables or waving a disapproving finger at him when things got out of hand. Such was the strange, touching paradox of Griffith, who had the timing and killer instinct of a panther but the emotional character of a frightened, dependent little boy.

After boxing legend Gil Clancy brought Griffith to his newly purchased Times Square Gym to train, Griffith discovered the shuffleboard arcade in the subway station at 42nd Street and 8th Avenue and the triple-feature-movie houses along 42nd Street. He also discovered the Blarney Stones and other pubs where drinks were cheap and the clientele came from a wide array of ethnic and class backgrounds. "I'd go home to Queens by taxi," he told me sheepishly, "never figuring there was any other way. Until my mama stopped me wasting all that cash and learned me how to get there by train."

Later on, Times Square became the place where Griffith squandered a good share of the purses he won, when he wasn't using the rest of it to support a vast array of brothers, sisters, aunts, uncles, cousins, his mother, and his "adopted" son. But by then, Times Square was becoming home to more and more "crazy shits." Adolescent loose cannons from the Bronx, Brooklyn, and Harlem were invading Griffith's haunts on 8th Avenue. They'd stow a duffel bag in a locker at Port Authority, then sleep in its men's rooms a few hours during the night or doze in pay-by-the-hour hotels or movie theaters. They'd try their hand at drug dealing or hustling at peep shows and pass time hanging out in the bars.

The scene had changed a lot, but Griffith held on. At his favorite bars, he'd play unofficial bouncer, breaking up fights when things got out of hand. "Sit down, Champ. We got people paid to keep order here," Kathy Hogan would holler. "But Emile would pop up anyways and smack 'em," Hogan told me. "And then he'd keep going at 'em just to prove that he was still in top shape."

In the several hustler bars both Griffith and I frequented, I witnessed several incidences when an obviously inebriated Griffith got dangerously out of control. Usually it was a petty situation in which he felt an adolescent homeboy hadn't shown the proper respect. His face contorted into a mask of anger, and you could see the rage coursing through his entire body. It took two men on each arm to hold him back from lunging at the object of his fury. Seeing this, it wasn't hard to imagine how the same energy had led to the death of Paret in the ring more than thirty years earlier.

Troublemakers who bumped into Griffith, however, could sometimes be considered lucky. After his own career in boxing ended, he'd begun training other fighters in Times Square and in New Jersey. He had a talent for channeling youthful rage and apathy into discipline and lethal fists. Later, he would handle such stellar fighters as Bonecrusher Smith and Juan LaPorte. Throughout his years as a trainer, he plucked adolescents from the streets and took them to the Times Square Gym. Whether it stuck or not, they appreciated the attention.

When Griffith walked up 8th Avenue, he was treated as something halfway between a messiah and a mark. The boys shouted, "It's the Champ!" trailing behind him and begging for a chance to fight or at least a dollar for a slice of pizza and a coke. More times than not, Griffith would hand money out to everybody, then spend the rest of it at a hustler joint surrounded by pals, protégés, and sycophants. The money would flow, and so would the booze.

"Kathy would take me into the men's room and empty all my pockets," Griffith told me. "I tried to hide some of it, but she always found the secret compartments. She'd give part of the cash to the bartender for drinks and hold all the rest for safekeeping. If I was a troublemaker that night, she always threatened to telephone Mama." One call to Griffith's mother could send him back to his bar stool, lowering his voice to a meek whisper.

By the early nineties, survival opportunities for Times Square homeboys were diminishing. Not only some of the Manhattan boxing gyms, but a lot of the all-night movie houses, peep shows, and hustler bars were gone. The Port Authority lockers had been dismantled, and no one could hang out in the terminal after midnight. Renovation was in the air, and the usual dealing spots were being raided on a regular basis.

Pushed into smaller and smaller territories, the homeboys hung on, but the mood of the place had gotten sinister. One summer night in 1992, Griffith found himself in Times Square with eight hundred-dollar bills in his pocket. He and fighter Juan LaPorte, whom he was training, had just returned from a bout in Australia. "I stopped for a few beers at La Fleur, a bar on 42nd Street where I used to work as a bouncer," Griffith told me. He couldn't remember the brutal beating in the adjoining parking lot that happened afterward, but the doctors had said it must have involved a baseball bat. It damaged his kidneys and sent him into intensive care. For several months, I didn't see him. He was hovering near death in a nearby hospital; but then, miraculously, he recovered.

Griffith's mugging marked a turning point not only for him but also for the neighborhood. A couple of years later, the building housing the Times Square Gym was demolished. All but two of Griffith's drinking haunts were raided and closed or bought out by the city. One surviving bar still had a much-reproduced, signed photo of the Champ taped to the wall, but Griffith's visits to the neighborhood had dwindled to a minimum.

The last time I saw Emile Griffith was in late 1998, sitting at Kathy Hogan's club as if times hadn't changed a bit. He and Hogan were laughing about a night twenty-eight years ago when the Champ had showed up in his new Lincoln Town Car, wearing a lynx coat and carrying his miniature poodle. "Kathy peeled off that coat quick and put it in the basement for safekeeping," said Griffith with a snicker. "Then Emile disappeared and didn't come back for a couple of weeks," added Hogan. "I took that poodle home with me and when Emile came for it, I told him it was mine!"

Griffith guffawed at the memory and ordered another Cuba Libre. One more certainly wouldn't hurt. He probably wouldn't be back up here for a long time, he said. "I'm hiding out until I see what the renovations bring," he added. "One thing I'm certain of is that it had to happen. This neighborhood's like a house that you fix and you fix. When you feel like you're going to fall through the floor, you get rid of it. You don't want to find yourself lying in the rubble."

He was right. A few years afterward, the police would close even Kathy Hogan's bar. The changes taking place in Times Square were unstoppable, but so were those in Griffith's life. A few weeks after our last conversation, I heard that his beloved mother had died. Kathy told me that without his mom alive, Emile had given in to an urge to return to his birthplace, the Virgin Islands. I never saw him again.

The Not-So-Secret Life of Consuela Cosmetic

Consuela Cosmetic was a bundle of contradictions, just like many people I know. She was a pre-op transsexual close to six and a half feet tall, who favored haute-couture apparel. She searched perpetually for the one person who didn't want something from her, although she wanted something from everybody she met. She was driven by impulses and appetites but claimed to have no patience at all for people with slovenly appearances or those who had not remade their lives under the most rigorous of discipline.

On a suffocating summer night in 1995, I watched her walk regally up a curving staircase to the Carter Hotel on West 43rd Street, to her birthday celebration at the drag club Sally's II. She was razor-thin by then, wasted by HIV. Over mile-long, matchstick legs she wore a dress of pink vinyl cinched at the waist, pushed out by a stiff, ruffled petticoat as if it were a leather flower. Her wig was a cascade of platinum. A film crew on its first day of shooting *Mirror, Mirror,* a documentary about her, followed close behind. Although she didn't know it at the time, she had exactly eight more months to live.

Those eight months would forever change the lives of three people: the film's British director-producer, Baillie Walsh; its French line producer, Claire Barnier; and Cosmetic's best friend and coactor in the documentary, Hector Xtravaganza. By the time the film was finished, all three weren't sure whether they'd made the film or the film had made them. Shooting had taken on the momentum of an act of nature. Consuela Cosmetic's documented last eight months had become a parable about the limits of fantasy and will power; and Walsh, Barnier, and Xtravaganza had become Cosmetic fantasies.

Consuela Cosmetic never became genitally female. For those unfamiliar with the transgender world, suffice it to say that there are various degrees involved—from cross-dressing to the use of hormones and implants, all the way to the surgical construction of genitals of the opposite sex. None holds sway over any other. Each has its admirers and its conveniences. Like the genders under which we all labor, each degree has its limitations. Cosmetic had large breast implants, but she chose not to alter her genitals, which were, in fact, one of the tools she occasionally used for survival. I had first seen her in a pornographic film that took the viewer into a gender-fuck hall of mirrors more than a year before meeting her, and I couldn't forget it.

In the film, a conservative-looking businesswoman leaving her office after hours is stopped by an African American female guard holding a flashlight and a nightstick. The guard is menacing and surly, statuesque and towering, in a skirted uniform and black police gloves. What starts as an argument over the businesswoman's right to be in the building after work turns into sadistic lesbian sex. The guard sexually tortures the businesswoman to "teach the white bitch a lesson." The businesswoman begins to like it; then the guard's hoisted skirt reveals an unexpected feature. But this is nearly outdone both by the believable persona and the face of the actor: Consuela Cosmetic's face had been fantastically altered by cheek and chin implants, multiple nose jobs, and perhaps jawline shaving. It was a pale, heavy-lidded African mask of oversized feminine proportions, sultry and heart-shaped, a testament to her rich fantasy life and imaginative aesthetic talents.

She was, in addition, a magnificent couturier, who designed and sewed for herself and many of the other queens who frequented Times Square. She could downplay her tall frame and ample breasts with conservative suits or pump them up with rich fabrics that clung to her like paint and produced a look of surreal glamour. It depended upon the occasion.

Film director Baillie Walsh first met her in a Times Square club on one on his trips to New York from London. He was bowled over by her unique showmanship and her provocative public image. Everyone noticed Consuela. She towered over all the other queens. Regardless of how you approached her, she was never at a loss for repartee. She had a fantastic array of costumes and a brazen social manner.

Walsh began writing a script that would feature her as a central character. Its working title was *Nine-and-a-Half Functional,* a phallic reference lifted from the transsexual escort ads in *Screw* magazine. The film would feature separate journeys for three very different characters in the New York area, all of whom would come together at the end. Catherine Deneuve and Carrie Fisher were slated to play the other two roles.

Walsh returned to New York in 1995 with funding from Premiere Heure, the French company that produced *Pigalle* and would later produce *Artemisia* and a film by John Maybury about Francis Bacon called *Love Is the Devil.* Right away, Walsh discovered that things had changed radically: Consuela Cosmetic was visibly ill. Her arms looked like a skeleton's; her breast implants dangled from a bony ribcage. London had become a ghost town for Walsh before he left it; two of his friends had just died of AIDS. He'd had no idea he was walking into the same scenario in New York.

Walsh realized Cosmetic would never be able to act in the film, but that didn't curtail his belief in what he called her "magical powers." He easily persuaded Premiere Heure's Patrice Haddad to detour the money for the script into a documentary about Cosmetic. Walsh agreed to take no salary. The film would be "about life, not death," he vowed, and about "a person living with AIDS." Little did he know what he was getting into. Consuela Cosmetic had come to a moment of reckoning in her life. As desperately as she still wanted the fantasy of glamorous womanhood, she also wanted the bitter truth. As a longtime exhibitionist, she wanted it for all to see.

When Baillie Walsh decided to make his film, he unconsciously placed himself in a classic dilemma. He was an outsider depicting a closed world. Voyeurism would get him nothing except a bad piece of sociology. Empathy, without participation, would at best produce a missionary's melodrama. Yet becoming part of The Life was like diving into a black hole of need, especially at the moment when Cosmetic's health was failing.

On July 6, 1995, Walsh took the plunge. His only protective gear was an ability to "become egoless" and enter fully into the fantasy lived twenty-four hours a day by a Times Square transsexual. So he dropped the role of auteur and rode his film like a rudderless boat for eight months, going wherever the crashing waves took him—which was into the realm of unflinching, visceral documentary.

"The reality of the film's emotions went way beyond what I'd thought film was," Claire Barnier told me. Gradually, she and Walsh had become instruments of Cosmetic's magic world of illusions. At the same time, they were vessels of her terminal confession—a passionate, somewhat sullen attempt to reveal the life of the street transsexual for what it really was. The result was a luscious, disturbing documentary called *Mirror, Mirror*—whose subtitle was *Limitation of Life*, a tongue-in-cheek reference to the great Douglas Sirk tearjerker, *Imitation of Life*. It was a repetitive, revolving-door trip between the gorgeous world of transvestite glamour—high-fashion lip-synch performances filmed in crisp 16 mm—and the shocking video revelations of someone who'd opted for a life of fantasy, no matter the awful price. Juxtapositions created heartbreaking ironies:

Cosmetic's gala birthday celebration was montaged with the sinister Midtown street outside, a world of peepshows and lurkers and cold passersby. Other scenes hit the viewer with clinical imagery that stunned and amazed: there was, for example, the scene of an operation, the documentation of Cosmetic's determined experiment to move back in the direction of manhood by the risky removal of her breast implants, surgery from which she almost didn't awaken. All was revealed, from the excruciating pain of a facial waxing and an illegal loose silicone–injection session to her work as a transvestite call girl. But the so-called ugly truth took second billing to the urgent beauty of Cosmetic's willful self-creation. It is a beautiful film. Over and over, we are swept back into the synthetic wonders of life as daydream and performance—breathtaking musical sequences that glisten with sequins and shiny feathers, heartfelt pantomimes of diva gestures that reveal all the emotional nuances of songs. Why can't it always be that way? Then, the outside world returns inevitably, often opposing the fantastic personal universe of Cosmetic yet sometimes enhancing it.

Consuela Cosmetic's determination to burst bubbles was rare in the world of the street transsexual. The nights of Times Square had always been about war against gloom. Glitter versus extinction. As darkness and decay swallowed everything around them, night people popped out like bright, defiant hallucinations. Their look was always brazen and confrontational. Their faces were set, but souls leaked out of eyes like faucets. Performance, costumes, and drugs kept up spirits. For people playing against the odds, negativity was a lethal downer. Cosmetic's deadpan admissions in *Mirror, Mirror* would deeply disturb some of her peers. Her transsexual friend Gina Germaine, who appears in the film, left the screening glassy-eyed and disappointed at "its arrogance of death. Consuela was getting her last shade," she complained. "Everybody said she was like that, but that wasn't how I saw her."

But Cosmetic's close friend Hector Xtravaganza, who was a part of the film almost from the beginning, had little sense of disillusionment about the real Consuela Cosmetic. He was an alumnus from the House of Xtravaganza, one of the Harlem drag-ball houses of fashion and voguing, which is portrayed in the film *Paris Is Burning.* Immensely talkative and articulate, he is, in his own words, "a butch queen," a male-identified gay—although he has flirted a great deal with drag, mostly in performance. For several years, he's had a secure full-time job, but in his younger, poorer years, when he was closer to the culture of the street, he'd found that "doing drag shows was a way to make some money, especially since I didn't want to be a prostitute." Still, each time the needle of estrogen became a looming possibility, Hector had pulled back. "Mother Angie told me," he said, referring to the deceased Mother of the House of Xtravaganza, "that you can't start thinking of these queens as women, no matter how glamorous they are, how beautiful." The death of Hector's best friend, Consuela, as well as his being in the film had made him see things "as they really are," all the negative sides of nightlife, the fact that "everybody's there to share the wigs and glamour, but when you fall and cry, you cry alone."

Hector Xtravaganza believed that Consuela began to feel trapped in her identity, burdened by having to sustain the illusion. He said she deeply resented normal women, gays, and even "butch queens" like himself. "You butch queens can go in and out of it when you want to," she told him with great bitterness. "It just isn't fair."

Highly resourceful and deeply distrustful, Cosmetic came up the hard way, or, as Hector Xtravaganza put it, "without any time between realizing she was a gay male and becoming a transsexual." The "parents" she spoke about in stories that changed from day to day were apparently a southern California minister and his wife, who cared for her after her blood parents passed away. When they were offered her ashes after her demise, they politely refused, explaining: "We didn't adopt her. She adopted us."

To know her was to accept being victimized to a certain extent. I can testify to that. I often ran into her in clubs and worked with her on some small films and videos, but we rarely socialized. When we did, I was the one spending money: "What you gonna do for me today?" seemed like her constant refrain. And what I saw as minor complications could deeply disappoint her. For example, she asked me to appear in the film by having me bring her a copy of a will. That encounter is recorded: the disappointment appears on her face when she discovers that the document I've brought is not a real will, which she's heard one needs to get cremated, but a living will, a kind of assurance against social control she feels too street smart to ever need.

Accordingly, part of the triumph of *Mirror, Mirror* is the filmmakers' ability to accommodate a difficult personality.

To a great extent, Walsh and Barnier put themselves at the mercy of Cosmetic's rhythms and demands for eight whole months. They became familiar with her love affairs and medical procedures, endured her mistrust and abuse. They paid her a salary, visited her in the hospital, and took her to buy a fur coat. At the beginning, however, Walsh's expectations stood between him and the pure medium of documentary. He could picture, he thought, how the film would end. At some point, he would have had enough, and a closing message would read, "Consuela Cosmetic is still fighting AIDS." Instead, shooting went on and on, sometimes in 16 mm film and other times in video, often without a crew, dictated by the curves of Cosmetic's last months and her waning health, by the amazing spectacle of her will to self-determination, no matter how physically wasted she became. It was as if the film had started making itself.

"My husband" or "my boyfriend" was how Cosmetic began to refer to Walsh during the filming. A transformation was taking place. Cosmetic had distrusted and resented white professionals; most of the ones she knew were paying tricks. Walsh had started out like the rest of them—wanting something from her. Now he was realizing her most cherished ambition. Through craft and caring, he was making her a star.

Meanwhile, both Walsh and Barnier had fused with the personality of Consuela Cosmetic. The involvement was probably a test of the sanity and ego strength of both. Because Cosmetic was deeply in love with Walsh, Barnier had started out in Cosmetic's mind as a dangerous rival—a "real" woman who was even lucky enough to come from Paris. But when they met, Barnier's casual way of dressing and lack of makeup and manicure seemed to infuriate Cosmetic. She couldn't understand how a woman could neglect to groom the body parts she herself so coveted. Then time passed, and Cosmetic's illness progressed. One by one, the members of her Times Square community dropped out of the picture. Only Xtravaganza, Walsh, and Barnier stood faithfully by her. The film became the central event in Cosmetic's life.

Cosmetic may have been able to tell it like it is to the camera, but she never lost her taste for illusion. She was a control freak. She'd stop at nothing to subjugate her environment and her body to her will. Her frank, sometimes gruesome descriptions of her bold body modification strategies (she punctured her breast implants with a hypodermic needle to make the doctors think they were rejecting in order to get the removal surgery paid for) were a kind of performance in themselves. Walsh's intuition told him that they weren't the kind of performances she'd ever want to review. She left them in the confessional of the film and moved on. The only parts of the film he ever showed her were some magnificent musical sequences she essentially directed herself and starred in, at her apartment. These she played on her VCR over and over, ecstatically pleased by their professionalism. The real subject of the film—the thin membrane between fantasy and the "world"—was never shoved in her face.

Ugly reality intruded, however, after her death, when Barnier began investigating the legal issues around the music in the film. All of it is incidental—music played in clubs to which the performers are lip-synching. However, Barnier soon discovered that it might be necessary to inquire about the music rights. When she did, in most cases, those who owned them refused to grant them. So Barnier sent their managers a tape, after which most were willing to negotiate. Unfortunately, the permissions fees threatened to total more than the cost of production. Then even worse difficulties loomed: out of all the performers contacted, two still stubbornly refused to grant music rights on any terms: Barbra Streisand and Richard Carpenter (Karen Carpenter's brother). Because of these difficulties, a superb documentary never got distributed.

Even so, the film continued to shoot itself, even after it was finished. It was as if Cosmetic's gargantuan will had begun to control every turn of event—even after her death. She'd decided to move back to California, which she extolled as a lost paradise and a new beginning. Over a period of weeks, she grew more and more emaciated as she neatly packed her possessions in an endless series of cardboard cartons. On the day her plane was supposed to leave, the cable man came to pick up her cable box and she handed the key to her empty apartment to her landlord. One of the last scenes in the film shows a tearful Xtravaganza accompanying the skeletal though smartly dressed Cosmetic to the airport.

At the airport, her plane was evacuated because of engine trouble. When a second threatened not to leave the ground, she walked off it and called Xtravaganza. He told her to come back to his house. She died in New York on March 6, 1997, a little more than a day later, exactly eight months after Walsh had started the film. In her carry-on bag were a typewriter and exactly eleven hundred dollars in cash. Xtravaganza, Walsh, and Barnier—who were with her to the end—went to Redden's Funeral Home to arrange for her cremation. The clerk was fastidious and picky, totaling up every little charge, from the car to the cremation center in New Jersey to the cardboard box in which the body would be transported. The total came to exactly eleven hundred dollars. It was eerily as if Consuela Cosmetic—self-made woman—had taken care of business until the very end.

3

Toward
the New Degeneracy

Toward
the New Degeneracy

Degenerates are not always criminals, prostitutes, anarchists, and pronounced lunatics; they are often authors and artists.

Max Nordau, *Degeneration,* 1892

So there was a new breed of adventurers, urban adventurers who
drifted out at night looking for action with a black man's code to fit
their facts.

Norman Mailer, "The White Negro," 1957

I

What are the compromises of the new witch hunt? This was
the question I asked myself in 1979 as I sat editing the "evolution disclaimer." This was a stamp to be applied to every
sixth-grade science book adopted by the state of Texas. It
admitted that the textbook discussed Darwin's theories of

Originally published as *Toward the New Degeneracy: An Essay* (New York: Edgewise,
1997).

evolution but denied that this was in any way an annulment of the theory of Adam and Eve.

Such an addition to the book promised to be Midas's touch. Winning the approval of the Texas school system meant seven-figure profits for the publisher. Every copy of the book sent to Texas could be stamped, but the disclaimer did not have to appear on shipments going to the more liberal states. Complicating this bizarre commercial and ideological enterprise even more was the actual text inside the book. For over four months I'd carefully edited the manuscript, obeying a specially prepared list of nonracist, nonsexist words that now made some passages read like a software-run translation from another language. In fact, three entire units used only plural pronouns because the nonsexist appositive "he or she" would lengthen sentences and drive up the reading level.

How had these two absurd agendas from the Right and from the Left—one blurring claims about human prehistory from apes and the other softening descriptive language about living humans—come together? Years later I had ceased to wonder. My textbook, which also had a chapter on the reproductive system, but no "he's" or "she's," was the precursor of a new conspiracy between two former enemies. Each had its grievances against the other, yet each agreed about the need to promote certain community standards.

Today we live the full flowering of that centrist paradise. Though nobody admits it, textbooks that simultaneously satisfy creationist beliefs and avoid sexist language are the "one-size-fits-all" of a very specific class. One main objective of these books is not to inform but to soothe tensions of difference and create the illusion of community. But the basic atoms of the structure of this community are the nuclear family, an element proven to be highly unstable. The fact that the family is now seen by everyone as the building block of the social order is why even the Left sees no psychoanalytic irony in gay lib T-shirts reading, "Hate Is Not a Family Value." Neither Left nor Right can admit how hate and resentment keep the nuclear family's incestuous urges tensely leashed. No one points to the many instances in which the goals of family and community are set against other members of society.

Thirty-three years ago nobody could have convinced me that any particular class could covertly form a strong coalition in America or that the agendas of the Left and the Right could ever be confounded with each other in the promotion of a single monotonous style of community life. At the time, I sleepwalked through a counterculture existence on public welfare in the hippie Haight-Ashbury. My life was one of glaring contradictions: I would purify my blood with macrobiotics and ginseng root but poison it with hallucinogenic toxins and frequent bouts of gonorrhea. Because I was void of ambition and virtually out of contact with the conventional workaday world, I thought that world was practically extinct. But my disdain for the material comforts of middle-class life never encroached upon my unending hunger for instant gratification. And I never understood how similar my impulses were to those of other consumers.

How could I have guessed that my sexual freedom would become shrouded by condom-consciousness? How would I have known that my hippie friends' nostalgia for rural space would become the activism of the block association and its sullen war against street people? Who would have dared to suggest that the fight for sexual rights could come to include a crusade against sexual abuse relying upon Victorian ideals of child protection? Or that violent campus uprisings would give birth to grievance committees that haggled over the crimes of politically incorrect speech? I didn't, but perhaps it was because I had never considered the class context in which the supposedly seismic changes of the sixties occurred.

My counterculture movement was a half-child of the Beat phenomenon that came before it and was thwarted. What made this phenomenon a foregone conclusion just a decade later was its profound connection to the city—just at the time when the next generation was being inculcated with the values of suburban life. Hipsters were attracted to the black jazz and intravenous drug subcultures of cities. They themselves came mostly from backgrounds that had nothing to do with these urban elements. Their niche was small and unstable— and hostile to the middle class but alienated from the working class because of the failures of thirties socialism.

In *Down and In: Life in the Underground*, Ronald Sukenick describes the Beats' early colonization of Greenwich Village, under the disapproving gaze of the neighborhood's Italian working-class toughs. No one who faced the grim reality of low income but had hopes of improving his condition saw anything romantic about forfeiting opportunities for education or employment. To find soul mates, the hipsters took a detour around the working class in search of those whose goals were short term, pleasure oriented, and anti-work.

In 1957 Norman Mailer wrote his notorious definition of the hipster in an essay called "The White Negro." The piece was a follow-up to a provocative statement he had sent to journalists and leading writers such as William Faulkner, suggesting that what Southern whites most feared about the black man was his sexual potency. "The White Negro" was a corollary of this proposition. It boasted that the hip white nonconformist was a voluntary "psychopath," whose attitudes and lifestyle mirrored those of the alienated American black. This idea was almost as repugnant when Mailer suggested it as it is by today's politically correct standards. In the black man, Mailer had attempted to locate all that was libidinal, rebellious, spontaneous, amoral, and infantile: all the impulses that make self-gratification the highest priority of the creative person and delayed gratification the province of the Square. Because these libidinal energies seemed so at odds with the current values of the decade in which Mailer was writing, he spoke of them using the sensationalized and morbid term "psychopath." Little did he know that just a decade later, the same loose id would be recast as a state of "higher consciousness" and instant gratification would be lauded as a groovy pursuit.

Mailer's use of "psychopath" was, in fact, deliberately obnoxious. It was an attention-getting tactic for a worldview that was more than willfully amoral. Being a "White Negro" meant accepting "the terms of death" and living with "death as immediate danger" at the dawning of the age of the atom bomb. It was a consciousness that urged one "to explore that domain of experience where security is boredom and therefore sickness," an attitude that so clashed with the optimistic tone of the times that it forced the "bohemian and the juvenile delinquent [to come] face-to-face with the Negro, and [made] the hipster a fact in American life."

The dropouts of the sixties who flocked to San Francisco may have been inspired by the hip "psychopaths" of the fifties, but they were curiously nonurban and very picky about the aspects of the down-and-out life to which they were willing to relate. They came mostly from middle-class white suburban homes and isolated nuclear families. They did not, as a rule, mix with the leather-jacketed working-class juvenile delinquents who were the other alienated youths of their time. The hippies wanted their lives to be a sensory bath that would make up for the monotony of the suburbs without sacrificing some of its conveniences, but their vision of the sensory was a living-color spectacle inspired by television and film. Perhaps the aspect of Beat culture that most inspired their split-level minds was the landscape of the open highway, promoted by Kerouac.

Unlike the Beats, whose philosophical tone was colored by European café existentialism and by the old dichotomy between the avant-garde and the bourgeoisie, the hippies of the sixties believed that heavy intellectualizing hampered creative and spontaneous behavior and that art sprang from the popular culture that they already liked. Their underground found its easiest outlets for spontaneity and pleasure in things that had mass appeal. This led to a self-destructing alliance with the mainstream. "During the sixties and seventies," writes Sukenick in *Down and In,* "the middle class and the counterculture fell into a complicitous pseudo-populism, which in any case is the main phony mode of American politics. The major message of pseudopopulism seems to be that what is good for the middle class is good for the people, while the needs of actual people, middle class or otherwise, are ignored in the name of populism." The "main phony mode" would also become a major field for commentary for avant-garde artists, as typified by Warhol's cynical embrace of pop. Sukenick feels, at any rate, that complicity with the middle class is the fate of any American vanguard movement, since the middle class claims to be only a "situation incidental to capitalist economics" and is willing to absorb any culture with profit potential that comes along.

The shift away from heroin toward psychedelics during the sixties emphasized the spiritual potential in the use of drugs. But it also cleansed the underground of its links to the ghetto and to crime. Mailer's extended simile of the White Negro was offensive to members of the new generation. In the first place, they found it glaringly racist to locate any particular set of qualities at all within a particular race. And to flower children it seemed perverse, as well, to suggest that a life devoted to pleasure could be nothing but destructive and dark. What is more, they weren't as pessimistic as the Beats, who implicitly assumed that they could not easily succeed in upsetting and reshaping social norms. What wasn't apparent at the time was that the vibrant new culture of the sixties was politically ineffectual, because it was unconsciously interested in middle-class opportunities. It was a consumer subculture, boasting greatly original personal styles, but with little power to change the monolithic institutions of America.

Within the decadent playpen of the sixties mind, some of the West's most eccentric personal quests were carried out. New frontiers of sexual identity, ancient pagan rituals, Eastern approaches to death, and new uses of drugs flourished like outlandish weeds. Genius became a perfection of lifestyle and was decidedly nonliterary. Art ceased to be isolated from the artist's sexual tastes, personal fantasies, clothing, or interest in drugs; the cult of personality took on crucial importance. The movement grew to include a larger and larger segment of the middle class, until suddenly even the most radical dropouts found that they were no longer in a meaningful adversarial position. They were safely included in the American economy and American mind.

In those naive days I still saw my lifestyle as a potent revolt against the monogamous sexual couple, the dynamics of the nuclear family, and the working world. What I didn't realize at the time was that the random couplings I so enjoyed could sometimes result in a real dyad—be it heterosexual or homosexual, with all its conventional aspirations of fidelity, family dynamics, and isolation from the Other; that my idealization of spontaneous "childlikeness" was an acceptance of the cult of the child, invented for the Victorian family and rife with covert strategies for diminishing the power and danger of childhood energies; or that my impulsiveness could be harnessed to consumerism. What I also hadn't realized is that the alternative existence I sought had already been described and condemned several times by bourgeois spokesmen in the war against degeneration.

In 1892 Max Nordau, a Jewish Hungarian journalist living in Paris, began a strangely personalized war against that era's counterculture lifestyles. In a book titled *Degeneration,* he launched an attack upon the Symbolists and those who in the future would be known as Expressionists, whose mentality he claimed was irrational, pessimistic, impulsive, darkly naturalistic, subversive, mannered, unresolved, solipsistic, experimental, and hyperaesthetic. To combat these degenerates, Nordau stressed simplicity, classical art forms, clear-headedness, materialism, physical culture, strength of will, the natural sciences, and bourgeois morality. In other words, he single-handedly tried to keep the revolution of Modernist sensibility from happening.

Today the rhetoric of Nordau's claims seems preposterous and obscene, with its reliance upon biology as the cause of most unconventional behavior; but his writings were taken seriously and even highly acclaimed until World War I, after which it became apparent that the aesthetic styles and philosophical stances against which he railed were to forge the basic tenets of twentieth-century avant-garde thought. Also, Freud's theories had begun to shed ridicule on the old ideas about a correlating physical cause for all mental problems. By the 1920s this once-famous critic had sunk into complete obscurity. Yet, today we find many of the attitudes in Nordau's middle-class doctrine echoed in the new emphasis on organic causes of mental disorders as diverse as schizophrenia and depression, on clean living through diet and exercise, on accessible art for the masses, and on the preeminence of family values.

Nordau's claims are cast in a Darwinian framework such

as would be absurd and repulsive today. He believed that the abnormal behavior of the degenerate was the product of a biologically inferior or organically damaged mind that could even be recognized in certain subtle body deformities and that the process of natural selection would weed out degeneracy over the course of generations. He also used evolution as a rationale for opposing political revolution, claiming that since evolutionary change is gradual and needs no outside interference, governments will change naturally over time.

Nordau's philosophy was one of bourgeois sagacity rooted in biological purity. In a way, it was diametrically opposed to everything that Mailer would later idealize in the White Negro. Nordau's cause was taken up at various times by doctors, critics, and the French Communist party, all of whom, until World War I, saw him as an eminent crusader for progress and a champion in the war against decadence and regressive behavior. This was, at the time, a typically liberal point of view, for what distinguished liberalism then, and what ties that version to its present incarnation, is its class sensibility. Although the middle-class liberal of today may pride himself on a certain open-mindedness, he also believes in the main tenets of his class, which include rationality, willpower, discipline, and social and scientific progress. It is contemporary liberalism's emphasis on the nuclear family as the root of everything that is good that seems to be moving it closest to that provincial liberalism of the late nineteenth century, in which the goodness of the drawing room was thought to be inviolable.

Nordau's basic causes for degeneration of body and mind were eerily similar to those touted by today's antitobacco activists, self-help groups, natural food advocates, and ecology activists. He said that degeneration was caused by a poisoning of the body through the use of alcohol, tobacco, narcotics, and stimulants as well as the stress of city living and the toxins of industry. He thought these health hazards decayed the brain, leading to many perversions, including the preference for the aesthetic over the useful. He maintained, for example, that the pointillism of contemporary painters was caused by overexcited nerve vibrations and that the pessimism of the Naturalists was caused by the enervations of city living.

What these theories boiled down to, finally, was that all of the sober standards of middle-class life were essential to the very survival of the species. In such a scheme, Mailer's White Negro would have been branded Public Enemy No. 1. Nordau thought art was okay, as long as it served the middle-class community and could be understood by its most average members. It had to recycle time-honored classical forms and emphasize action, plot, and the moral message. Along this line, he became an early proponent of popism, maintaining that an entertainment that appealed to the common man had to be for the good of the community. His ideal art form was today's G-rated film with the happy ending.

In more than five hundred pages, Nordau belligerently described all of the characteristics of degeneration, proving, he thought, how it issued from minds organically debased by inferior inheritance and bad habits and demonstrating how degeneration poisoned the majority of artistic creations and design styles of his era. The beginning of the book set forth the symptoms, diagnosis, and etiology of the social disease that had infected culture. The last two chapters offered a prognosis and therapeutics for the cure.

The symptoms of the disease included overaffected clothing fashions, dandyish mannerisms, baroque fin-de-siècle salon interiors, Wagnerian chromatics, and Zolaesque wallowing in urban filth. Nordau catalogued all of these in a manner worthy of the decadent novel *A rebours* by Huysmans, an author who is one of the many pre-Modernists lambasted in Nordau's book. Nordau's diagnosis of the social illness of degeneration is also a condemnation of the "purely literary mind, whose merely aesthetic culture does not enable him to understand the connections of things, and to seize their real meaning." The "connections of things" were something that could only be thoroughly understood by scientists.

Mannered aesthetes, mystics, Symbolists, Decadents, Diabolists, Ibsenists, and Wagnerians were the White Negroes of Nordau's day. They suffered, according to him, not only from a kind of hysteria that often satisfies itself in verbal outpourings but also from certain physical markers of degeneration. Nordau borrowed this idea from noted biological determinists of his day and earlier, such as Franz Joseph Gall and Caesar Lombroso, to whom the book is dedicated. He reasoned that if he were given the opportunity to examine those suspected of degeneration, he would undoubtedly discover corresponding physical deformities. But the demands of privacy made this impossible, and it was not, in fact, called for, since "it is not necessary to measure the cranium of an author or to see the lobe of a painter's ear, in order to recognize the fact that he belongs to the class of degenerates."

If a degenerate became a novelist, reasoned Nordau, his narrator would be likely to confound right and wrong. Nordau had witnessed the avant-garde intellectuals of his day going to great lengths to show the relativity of questions of good and evil. He did not think such degenerates were blatant criminals, but he accused them of the nearly criminal act of trying to prove the "theoretical legitimacy of crime." They were borderline cases who should have known better, like Mailer's White Negroes. They "discover beauties in the lowest and most repulsive things." Like Mailer's White Negroes, they were characterized by an "unbounded egoism" and "impulsiveness," stigmatized by "emotionalism" and "pessimism," and disinclined to positive action. In fact, it was likely that many were disciples of Schopenhauer or practiced Buddhism. Add to this taste for mysticism, a predilection for flights of the imagination, an impressionable nature, and even "an irresistible desire . . . to accumulate useless trifles," a sickness Nordau dubbed the "buying craze," borrowing a term from the psychologist Valentin Magnan.

As has been mentioned, Nordau traced the etiology of the cultural disease of degeneration partly to poisoning through drug addiction, an attitude strangely prophetic of today's proponents of the war on drugs, who love to attribute our major social ills to the problem of urban drug abuse, with little reference to the vicissitudes of class and poverty or social or psychological conditioning. However, Nordau added a pre-Fascist biological imperative to his etiology, writing that "a race which is regularly addicted to narcotics and stimulants in any form (such as fermented alcoholic drinks, tobacco, opium, hashish, arsenic), which partakes of tainted foods (bread made with bad corn), which absorbs organic poisons (marsh fever, syphilis, tuberculosis, goitre), begets degenerate descendants who, if they remain exposed to the same influences, rapidly descend to the lowest degrees of degeneracy, to idiocy, to dwarfishness, etc."

To all the causes of degeneracy, Nordau added one other crucial influence: residence in large towns, pointing out: "Parallel with the growth of large towns is the increase in the number of the degenerate of all kinds—criminals, lunatics . . . ; and it is natural that these last should play an ever more prominent part in endeavoring to introduce an ever greater element of insanity into art and literature."

His alliance with the wholesome would backfire, of course. For though his insistence upon clean living and scientific thought jived with the values of the bourgeoisie, his theories about the link between physical and psychological degeneration would feed the Nazis' racial theories about Jews, of which Nordau was one. He died in 1923, without seeing the Holocaust, but not before it was hinted to his disadvantage that viciousness, degenerate tastes, and moral aberrations can fester and grow within a context of family values and physical purity. Still, one cannot stress how much his supposedly outmoded worldview resembles the one currently in vogue among today's centrist social critics in our media and government. These modern hygienists deplore the decay of the city, the corrosion of drugs, and the hazards of pollution as if they were evil entities independent of other conditions. They hold them up to middle-class models of mental, physical, and sexual health. They call for an end to urban crime but do not want to delve into the connected complexities of class or money. And they use the controlling cultural institutions of America, now located in the suburban lifestyle, as basic assumptions, similar to the way Nordau equated science with the rituals of the Victorian drawing room.

What Nordau, today's journalists and politicians, and, to some extent, Norman Mailer left out of their formulas about marginality was conceptualized in a radical way by one social scientist widely read during the 1950s and 1960s. His name was Oscar Lewis, and he is today almost as out of vogue as Nordau became. In 1966, at the time of the war on poverty, Lewis published *La Vida: A Puerto Rican Family in the Culture of Poverty—San Juan and New York,* a study based on Puerto Rican families from two slums of San Juan and their relatives in New York City. In this book and others, Lewis was bold enough to advance the theory of a universal culture of poverty, given the right economic and political conditions. His definition of the culture of poverty was based on eighty characteristics that he thought could be discovered in the slums of any modern nation, regardless of climate, race, or cultural heritage of those involved. Many of the individual psychological traits Lewis lists are characteristic of Mailer's glorified Negro, but Lewis took care to point out that "many of the problems we think of as distinctively our own or distinctively Negro problems (or that of any other special racial or ethnic group), also exist in countries where there are no distinct ethnic minority groups."

Lewis's characteristics also match many of Nordau's symptoms of degeneration. When one considers that Nordau's interest in degeneration was mostly a way of refuting the spontaneity, alienation, or pessimism of the avant-garde artists of the time, and that Mailer's White Negro was a way of restoring these qualities to white artists by encouraging them to emulate the urban black, a spiritual coalition between the culture of poverty and the culture of bohemia is revealed.

However, Lewis's position is seen today by many as a prejudicial indictment of the poor, with racist and classist overtones. The effrontery of assigning a cultural identity with psychological traits to a segment of the population caught in economic deprivation is interpreted as snobbism, as if one were saying: "We all know what those people are like." There is today an unspoken agreement among people of the media to pretend that everyone shares the same (middle-class) values and that some—either because of or in spite of individual character—are (temporarily) caught in unpleasant situations *or* have become inexplicably evil. If a woman in a housing project who smokes crack leaves her three-year-old child to starve for several days, the report on the evening news implies that she is different from us only in regard to this isolated action. It is as if a familiar middle-class persona were magically converted from Jekyll to Hyde, an event explainable in the terminology of drug abuse or crime but never in a cultural context that includes the values or economic variables of the perpetrator's community. Lewis was bold enough to suggest that economics and political control could create a lasting, uniform, inherited culture that was even more powerful than an inherited ethnicity and that this culture was a context in which these events so unusual to us took place. Lewis wished neither to romanticize nor indict the poor but merely to demonstrate that their culture was "an effort to cope with feelings of hopelessness and despair which develop from the realization of the improbability of achieving success in terms of the values and goals of the larger society." He also appreciated some of the positive aspects of the culture of poverty—the sensuality, spontaneity, sense of adventure, and indulgence of impulses that come from living in the present time. "Perhaps it is this reality of the moment which the existentialist writers are so desperately trying to recapture but which the culture of poverty experiences as natural, everyday phenomena," he went so far as to say, linking the metaphysics of the culture of poverty to those of the Modernist and the hipster.

Like Mailer's Negroes and White Negroes, and Nordau's degenerates, Lewis's members of the culture of poverty are contemptuous of the dominant institutions of middle-class life. They hate the police, mistrust government officials, and even feel a cynicism about the church. They are aware of middle-class values and may even espouse them, but they do not live by them. Their communities lurch along with a minimum of planning and organization, and individuals are apt to go where the day takes them. They have debunked the Victorian ideal of childhood as a state of protracted innocence by shortening the period of protection to which a child is entitled. Although they may claim strong family values, marriages tend to be consensual rather than legal, there is a high incidence of abandonment, and sibling rivalry is a constant threat to nuclear family functioning.

Sex fills a diverse set of needs for the members of the culture of poverty and encompasses pleasure, money, love, and machismo achievement. The incest taboo is less rigid in family life, and male children are sometimes erotically stimulated by mothers and other family members to develop pride in their erections. Nordau would not approve of such a family setting, but he would be more likely to link such behavior to biological inheritance or "poisoning" than to poverty. Mailer would approve, but he would find his causes in the sociology of race in America.

When reading Lewis, one must come to the conclusion that in respect to the poor's libidinal mentality, they are like bohemians. They "show a great zest for life, especially for sex, and a need for excitement, new experiences and adventures. . . . They value acting out more than thinking out, self-expression more than self-constraint, pleasure more than productivity, spending more than saving, personal loyalty more than impersonal justice." Certainly these qualities were familiar to anyone in fin-de-siècle Paris, in Beat San Francisco, or throughout the sprawling sixties underground.

The geographical interfacing of the culture of poverty and the "willfully poor" bohemian is familiar to us today in urban neighborhoods such as New York's East Village. Communities like the East Village begin when young, alienated newcomers arrive to superimpose a quirky and extemporaneous culture upon a traditionally immigrant neighborhood. Although the neighborhood will still be largely populated by the very poor (those too poor to object), the ones who come to take advantage of the situation are largely from middle-, working-, or upper-class backgrounds and are mostly white and often artistically inclined. Some are self-styled anarchists, and many are vociferously alienated from the American mainstream. They come not only in a search for cheap rents but because aspects of the culture of poverty suit their makeshift professional style, their chaotic schedules, and the openness of their sex lives. But even though the atmosphere of abject poverty facilitates the life of bohemia, the latter mixes with the former very little.

The locals respond with varying degrees of hostility to the greenhorns who come to create an underground just as the Italian working-class hoods described in Sukenick's *Down and In* gave the evil eye to West Village interlopers in 1948. The newcomers may emulate the fashions of the culture of poverty from a distance and certainly draw a charge from its noisy and chaotic energy on the street, but once bohemia takes root in a neighborhood, many of those who promoted it, who always had other options, and who are unconsciously inculcated with the middle-class values of their past, suddenly find themselves with changed allegiances. They change the terrain as they change, instituting block associations, co-ops, community police groups, and private day-care centers to combat the very insecurities that once attracted them.

This does not explain, however, why today's underground has produced less of an avant-garde—in literature, art, or fashion—than the late-nineteenth-century European culture of the cafés, which germinated Modernism; the Beats, who christened a new school of American literature and inter-faced with the Abstract Expressionists; or the hippies, whose rapport with mass culture shaped the entertainment and sex-ual mores of the seventies. The reason bohemia has lost its teeth today is because its energy source—its vital links with the culture of poverty—have been all but severed. The dull-ing of the counterculture edge began when the spontaneity, sexual promiscuity, and pop tastes of the hippies found too little a likeness in the energies of rejected people. By the eighties this attitude developed into the opportunistic alien-ation of the yuppies.

In fact, the very disorganization of the culture of pov-erty, which is the key both to its spontaneity and its quirky energy, frightened the hippies and the next generation of suburban exiles. Many came from homes where corpora-tions and civic institutions weren't mystifying faraway cabals. Their need for order and security was bound to rear its head. The symptoms in their split allegiances were there from the start in their linguistic style. They had a suburban fear of the exaggeration, boasting, and macho obfuscation of under-class communication. They never developed their own com-plete argot. Although hippie language did have its slang, this never differed much from the suburban language of the Val-ley Girl. Conversely, if one looks back a decade, it becomes clear that there was a time when Beat argot was so infused with the rhythms of jazz that it could barely be understood by outsiders. All the subversive values of the hip culture were encoded within it. The White Negro enjoyed a special link to urban ghetto culture, which kept him marginal but vital.

2

I grew up as the son of a lawyer in Syracuse, New York, a small suburban-style city with a population so median that it was a center for market-research testing of new products. When I came to New York's East Village in 1974, after four and a half years in San Francisco, I didn't understand that my counterculture ideology wouldn't be enough to keep me from beginning a descent into an identity crisis. My socially ambiguous existence as a marginal would gradually come to seem flaccid and ineffectual. This was perplexing to me because, on the surface, my pleasure-oriented activities had seemed a subversive dumping of my middle-class past.

In San Francisco I'd taken homosexual experiments to extremes. Several nights a week in the city's baths and back rooms had brought my total number of different sex partners into the thousands. Though I'd been writing fiction, I was unpublished and working in a proud, narcissistic vacuum. Up to that moment I had adamantly refused to use my rather paltry liberal arts education for any occupation or mode of communication that felt "professional."

There was something anticlimactic about the permissive climate of the mid-seventies, a hollow feeling about the libidinal prizes for which we had strived in the preceding decade. At the beginning, I'd been attracted by the new identity politics forming around sexual orientation. This came from the fact that I'd been galvanized as a teenager by John Rechy's *City of Night* and William Burroughs's *Junky* and was convinced that the political power of homosexuality lay in its implicit subversion of the daily life of the family. In 1969, in San Francisco and Berkeley, I'd joined the gay liberation movement and, appearing with matted hair and ripped jeans, helped picket homophobic radio stations, stage fuck-ins on church banquettes, and invade a convention of the American Psychiatric Association that was exhibiting an electrode shock machine used to convert homosexuals by aversion therapy.

Back then, I was under the quaint and happy impression that the homosexual was a powerful taunt to society's dearest assumptions. I was heartened by what I thought was homosexual privilege—the fact that our group defied the biological laws of succession and were thus the only group that could not be permanently eliminated: you could kill me, but not what I stood for, because my people didn't need gay mothers or fathers to be reborn. On the other hand, when genocidal Spaniards killed off all the Tainos on the island of Puerto Rico, they disappeared from the planet. When the Polish and German Jews were exterminated, it was obvious that it would take more than a generation to replace their numbers. As a group, homosexuals were luckier. They could never be eliminated for more than a generation, after which they would return again as the children of unwitting heterosexuals to mock the tyranny of progeny.

I also highly valued the experiential vigor of homosexual promiscuity. In a world in which middle-class people were increasingly shutting out other classes, the willingness to fuck opened class and age barriers. The gay world was a place where the retired doctor might adopt the street boy hustler or the Harvard student could find himself in bed with a forty-year-old mechanic. My sexual escapades had made me privy to lifestyles, class realties, and ethnicities most people of my background never encountered.

Why, then, this feeling of irrelevance as the seventies rolled by? Perhaps it was a foreshadowing of the limitations of identity politics. It would become apparent—a decade later—that a politics concerned with who you are is the politics of a particular class and that assimilated minorities—be they black, female, or gay—are only being offered a holding cell by being defined as a particular subculture of that class.

As the seventies progressed, identity politics would not only become the only politics of the Left, but it would be shaped by minorities within the educated classes, whose need for assimilation would recast subversive elements of society—homosexuals, ghetto inhabitants, or alcoholics—as normal people who participated at least mentally in wholesome middle-class life and were in need of protection and help. This was the legacy of the new "suburbanized" counterculture. John Rechy's homosexuals and the addicts of Hubert Selby Jr.'s *Last Exit to Brooklyn* had found solidarity among other addicts, transvestites, prostitutes, and petty criminals. Those shaped by identity politics would seek the approval of politicians, family members, corporations, and the clergy.

Identity politics turned the feisty, rageful dialectic of the Outsider into a polite multicultural tea party. It eventually drained discussions of race, gender, and sexual orientation of all irony and opportunities for humor because its entire rhetoric came from one protected cultural class. Lenny Bruce had understood the power of the epithet and its great opportunities for irony and parody. University grievance committees do not. Politically correct terms became a way of keeping difference at a respectful distance that amounts to denial, and labeling began to embalm what it described. Euphemisms like "people of color" sounded like "Mr." to me, who remembered a recent time when people had grown used to calling each other by their first names. The severing of the old, unspoken intimacy between the bohemian, the ghetto dweller, and the radical, which had started with the hippies, was completed by this new politics. Gay liberationists and feminists redefined the troublesome underclass, who reappeared only as bashers, batterers, sex objects who did not understand their oppression, or macho closet cases.

In formulating the new emphasis on identity and assimilation, the middle classes unwittingly conspired to strangle libido and lower-class expression. But I didn't understand this yet. Thinking of myself as a liberated homosexual, I continued to comb through the liberal gay papers, occasionally wondering why the articles seemed so repetitive. To avoid stereotyping, the journalists had self-censored most of the generalizations needed to talk about groups. One had to vehemently deny that gays were abnormal or different than anyone else, but one also had to insist on the necessity of our own books, magazines, and clubs. As these writers fumbled to locate a shared gay identity, they nervously tiptoed past any controversial pronouncements about gays. The resulting cultural discussion was total blandness, a concentration on fashion styles and modes of humor among homosexual men.

Malaise overtook me in the late seventies. I wanted to escape for even a moment from the pressures of my self-imposed identity, as well as my class, my family, the world. I found that escape momentarily in pornography, which today is the last allowable transgressive expression of today's bourgeois consciousness. For a few moments leading to orgasm, it was possible to evade Nordau's wholesome world of antiurban family wisdom, plain-spoken honesty, and non-fragmentary plots, a world that had expanded horrifyingly in contemporary times to co-opt its old enemies—removing the stigma Nordau placed on homosexuality, mental illness, or addiction in order to suck these marginals into a denatured pocket of the bourgeoisie.

The senseless, unreal prolongations of sexual energy on the video screen or in grimy porno theaters eclipsed worries about family protection and budget management. The amoral bath of lasciviousness suspended for a moment the march of progress. This mass-produced clinically revealed sex mocked Nordau's equation of science, reason, and bourgeois moderation, which was about to become so popular again as we neared the end of the next century.

Then came the sledgehammer. AIDS simultaneously ruined my momentary escapes from a decent curtailed identity and smashed the idea I had of promiscuity as an effortless expander of social consciousness. In the early eighties, before it was known exactly how AIDS was spread—before safer sex—I was catapulted into a panicked loss of a principal means of self-expression and contact with other humans.

Now fucking casually meant more than a flouting of middle-class standards and a mockery of middle-class hygiene. It meant illness and death—deterioration.

In the first years of the AIDS crisis, I turned my libidinal energy inward and converted it into obsessive self-examination of body and mind—as if I were looking within for proof of Nordau's degeneration. Being part of the AIDS risk group made me feel unclean, expendable, and marginalized, but I had no vehicle, no vibrant counterculture medium in which to express and share this sensation. As is evident from contemporary rhetoric from the Right, the AIDS paradigm can be easily shaped to fit Nordau's theories. He would have seen it as a sickness of the body that can be traced to the sexual appetite of a degenerated brain, which is exactly how some on the Right speak of it today.

However, on the Left, AIDS became part of other strategies. Ironic as it may seem, it was a powerful force in mainstreaming homosexuality. Families who would never have known that a member was gay were forced to confront homosexuality with tragic acceptance when a son or brother became ill. The liberal mind was bombarded with detailed descriptions of homosexual behavior by the medical profession and the media.

The mainstreaming of homosexuality was pushed along further by the new breed of activists. In fact, AIDS activism would prove to be the only salient and effective radical political movement of the eighties. National awareness about AIDS, women's special health-care needs, teenage sex, and sex education was brought to the forefront of popular cultural discourse by AIDS activism, which at the time may have seemed strident or unrealistic but actually did result in influencing the big pharmaceutical companies, government health programs, public education, and the FDA.

The new activists of the epidemic, specifically those of ACT-UP, were even more firmly entrenched in a particular class reality than the people of the sixties counterculture had been. ACT-UP's members were mostly white and highly educated and sometimes linked to insiders in advertising and the media. Despite ACT-UP's nonauthoritarian structure, its demonstrations were highly organized media events, which made ingenious use of fax machines, sophisticated graphics, and articulate speakers. However, I believe that the class orientation of most of the participants kept the AIDS movement from achieving more than a narrow focus. As women's issues, prison issues, race issues, and class issues came forward, the movement was fragmented and weakened.

AIDS escalated the absorption of homosexuality—at least temporarily—into the culture at large. But it left the true gay radical, the bohemian who hearkened back to the gay separatist past, more alone than ever before. The old-style gay bohemian resented the media, was intrigued by other class realities, and scorned intimacy with the mainstream. If he became HIV positive, the kind of support offered him by the AIDS establishment was likely to be repugnant to his values in some aspects. If he were negative, he found himself in the guilt-ridden position of feeling critical and contemptuous of such support.

When libido and experimentation have been curtailed within one subculture, the unrepentant bohemian may look elsewhere for energy. Those well-off radicals who rubbed shoulders with the working class in the thirties made their "descent" partly because they craved the simple, honest energy of hunger and anger—the energies of the culture of poverty. I found the objective correlative of my AIDS panic, self-doubt, and despair in the underclass culture documented by Oscar Lewis.

It began when the painter Scott Neary loaned me the 1983 novel *Saul's Book* by Paul T. Rogers. According to the short bio in the Penguin edition, the author of this first novel had been a schoolteacher and social worker; but after he was murdered by the Times Square hustler whom he had adopted and to whom he had dedicated *Saul's Book,* a cover article in the *Village Voice* revealed that Paul T. Rogers was very much like his character "Saul." He was a highly intelligent ex-con with one foot still in the embezzling underworld and an alcoholic and drug addict who frequented young hustlers.

Saul's Book is a pre-AIDS novel about the street life and street mind of a Times Square Puerto Rican hustler and heroin addict named Sinbad and his ongoing relationship with his Jewish trick, lover, and father figure, Saul. In Sinbad I sensed a much more vital and courageous version of my own despair about AIDS and lost identity. Making use of the skills of spontaneity, forgetfulness, impulsiveness, and casual generosity that Oscar Lewis detailed in *La Vida,* Sinbad manages to clothe his risk-filled life with the same flamboyant affectations and makeshift solutions that enraged Nordau and thrilled Mailer. As an underclass person he is, de facto, a person at risk. But instead of anguishing over his situation as I anguished in the mirror over blemishes, certain that they foretold illness and death, Sinbad launches into his sea of risk-filled pleasure with great élan and little self-preserving narcissism. In a perverse way, he symbolized all the courage in extremity that I lacked. In the age of AIDS I went on a voyage to find the world of Sinbad, hoping to recover that sense of the old "degeneration" that had once linked under-class energies with the underground avant-garde.

Saul's Book helped transform me from a fearful and de-moralized person who dabbled in writing into a driven writer on the way to becoming a novelist. A feeling of solidarity with the street people of Times Square, whom I began to associate with, gave me a way of incorporating my sense of being AIDS-endangered and expendable into an exciting literary endeavor. It also revived my hope of escaping the prison of my class and envisioning a new kind of countercul-ture. From then on, virtually all my writing was about the subject of underclass energy and the social comedy that is played out when middle-class people in search of that energy come in contact with it as voyeurs, reformers, pleasure seek-ers, or victims.

Little by little I began to realize that the malaise I had experienced before the AIDS crisis was due to the fact that bourgeois experience, encompassing my old homosexual identity, had been overcharted and was now laid out as neatly as the parking places at a strip mall. Beyond it was the unknown territory of the sexualized, drug-ridden street. Whereas Mailer had relied upon the medium of jazz and mar-ijuana to bridge a gap between the paucity of his own middle-class background and the exciting world of the street, I began to rely upon the only path of exchange left between the middle class and the underclass: prostitution and harder drugs.

I began hanging out in Times Square bars in 1984. By 1987 I was a familiar face in the neighborhood. I spent a significant part of my time with male prostitutes, struck up love affairs with ex-cons, financially supported a throwaway child who eventually went to a drug treatment program, and experimented with drugs myself. I'm not boasting about what may appear to resemble a descent, nor am I recommending it to those trying to confront their own fear and trembling. It is merely something that happened at a moment in my life when all seemed hopeless and likely to end in catastrophe.

My descent galvanized my writing as if I had been given private access to a secret and infinite cosmos. Times Square mentalities charged my texts with a raw sexual ambiance that flirted with death. My identification with the people of the street allowed me to immerse myself in monologues that I could imagine taking place in their voices and their mind frame.

In his book *Erotism* Georges Bataille writes that "only the anti-social underworld preserves a quantity of energy that does not go into work." Bataille also claimed that the compensation for the humdrum of daily life was provided in pre-democratic days by the obscenely exciting spectacle of royal privilege and in modern times by the spectacle of the wealthy European playboy or American gangster. This may be true, but in America there are few representations of criminal excess that do not rely upon the judgments of the police blotter or at least the sentimentality of the kitchen-sink drama.

Selby's *Last Exit to Brooklyn* is one of the beautiful exceptions. *Manchild in the Promised Land,* by Claude Brown, is another. The black exploitation novels of Iceberg Slim and Donald Goines are even better examples. However, in most cases, when the underworld is represented, the commercial exploitation of crime or weepy ethnic nostalgia overcomes all of the libido, energy, and aggression of Mailer's treasured "psychopaths" and attaches the hypocritical disclaimer of a moral message at the end. For those thinkers and artists seriously interested in the energies of the street, there are only three possible approaches: one is the sober documentation and analysis of underclass reality in the mind of a social scientist, like Oscar Lewis; another necessitates being born into these realities, as were Claude Brown and Hubert Selby Jr., and then miraculously pulling oneself up long enough to conceptualize degradation with honesty and rage; or, last, one can participate in these realities as an outsider, situating oneself somewhere between voyeur and victim.

As a middle-class person who wanted something from the street, I found that the more prudent and self-preserving I was, the more I became a voyeur, and the less emotionally valid my connection to, my enjoyment of, and consequently my writing about, this world. On the other hand, the more I participated and the more risks I took, the more libidinous and meaningful my connection to the world and my writing about it became.

However, participating in this world made it less likely that I would continue to write, as it entailed a heavy involvement in drugs, sex, risky ephemeral relationships, and petty criminal pursuits. I had to strike a very shaky balance between the stances of voyeur and participant to remain productive, which is not to say that I began to frequent Times Square for the purpose of writing a book. It was for the purpose of pleasure and because of despair that I found myself night after night in the company of junkies, crackheads, hustlers, and drag-queen prostitutes. As I began to write a novel about my experiences, which was eventually published as *User,* my role stabilized, and I became part voyeur, part exploiter, part chronicler, and part victim.

I didn't realize until later that the Times Square of those years was the perfect milieu for someone like me. It was then (but because of gentrification and Disney's new investments in property is no longer) the last crossroads of the classes in the old sense of "downtown," a central marketplace and neutral terrain where exchanges took place. Many of the people who came to buy drugs or sex in Times Square would not have dared to venture into the neighborhoods where those who sold these commodities lived. But in Times Square they had momentary, curtailed contact with these people, and I witnessed again some of the old miracles of promiscuity and class mixes that I had valued in the past. Accordingly, when a hustler was arrested, and I went to Rikers Island to post bail, the most surprising additional "friends" showed up; for, top designers, champion prizefighters, devoted husbands with children, and politicians were also part-time frequenters of this world.

It took me four years to collect my notes and get into the right frame of mind to write *User.* I took my notes in medias res, scribbling them on matchbook covers or napkins near the doors of the toilets in bars as crack smokers paraded in and out; at the bar counter, where fights sometimes erupted; sitting naked on the edge of beds in a pay-by-the hour hotel, after a trick had left; in after-hours clubs at dawn, where stoned queens and hustlers battled or made love; or on street corners, where I was sure to be hit up for one- and five-dollar bills by my so-called pals. This world of transactions was, in a perverse way, a fitting context for an exile from a counterculture that had distinguished itself by consumerism. However, here the players of the money game were the insiders, who belonged to "The Life," and the outsiders in search of pleasure, who served as their "marks," or victims, and were fleeced before ever being offered tangible goods.

In a world where aggression was only tensely leashed and private property depended upon who could get his hands on it, I discovered a surprising warmth and courage in the regulars. The street hood may be a loose cannon with rage and violence pulsing close to the surface, but his easy release of aggression leaves behind a kind of sweetness and generosity that the tight-assed bourgeois, full of pleasantries and buried resentments, never achieves. At the beginning, it amazed me when those bed partners, who radiated a childlike warmth, began to trust me enough to confess the violent crimes for which they'd done time. Suddenly, the vigor of their sexual caresses titillated me with other, frightening meanings, an ambiguity that they used to boost their moments of mastery over me, an exotic in their world. Likewise these people's early familiarity with physical pain, disappointment, and public institutions gave them the patience of fatalistic philosophers who could stomach rough treatment from medical personnel, suspicious behavior from sullen merchants, or long hours on bureaucratic lines that would drive most of us to distraction. It was clear that the muscular bodies they positioned within these many demeaning or risky social sites—welfare lines, police lineups, drug-dealing corners—were their sole asset, radiating great vitality and nervous pride. But there was a crushing irony between these bodies and the map of abuse drawn on them by the many scars and bruises. They were like vital, valuable goods that had been mishandled. Their statuesque brutality, liquid eyes, and exhibitionistic stances intrigued me more than the carefully conditioned and cleaned bodies of my own class.

Politics was virtually nonexistent on the street. But in prison, which I visited quite often as one favorite after another was rounded up by the police, politics was startlingly radical and alienated. I remember going to Fishkill Correctional Facility several times to visit a twenty-seven-year-old of Puerto Rican background whom I'd met by correspondence through another friend who was incarcerated. The twenty-seven-year-old had had a childhood of family violence and had been in prison for most of his adult life. Now he was often plagued by vicious nightmares of torture and witchcraft. Through courses in prison, he'd developed a high level of articulateness and was interested in revolutionary politics. This was during the Gulf War. He and his fellow inmates all supported Hussein. When I asked him why, he answered, "What has this country ever done for us?"

Through him and other inmates I learned about the Five Percenters, a politicized religious group developed and propagated in prisons during the seventies as one way of promoting Islamic culture. The name was based on the assertion that 85 percent of humanity is poor and uneducated and exploited by a controlling 10 percent. The remaining 5 percent, who are the Five Percenters, claim to be exempt from exploitation because of their spiritual knowledge and emotional strength. At a time when complacent materialists were jumping on the Reagan bandwagon, I found the loopy politics of my prison radical friends, whether reasonable or not, strangely refreshing.

Many who come from the culture of poverty and the street have stretched the boundaries of sexual identity in ways uninterpretable by middle-class liberationist paradigms. My young prison friend was straight-identified and always asked me for copies of *Penthouse,* but during collect calls and in letters he took the homosexual tease to so graphic an extent that the most liberated proponents of male middle-class consciousness-raising would be astonished or appalled. This was his way of paying me back with erotic stimulation for the books, clothing, or money I sent him. But why did he have such a sure intuition for what could arouse me?

Bisexuality in prison, on the street, and throughout much of the third world does not resemble that careful and philosophical bisexuality of our contemporary post-feminist, post-Freudian enlightenment. The street macho can be homophobic and intensely homosexual at the same time. The mixture of libido and flamboyant ego that spills out of the underclass male, as well as his familiarity with the skills of prostitution, make him available to both sexes in many instances. It's the role he plays that matters, regardless of which sex he does it with. The conditions of the culture of poverty—early sexual initiation, parents with multiple partners, and overcrowded living conditions in which siblings share the same bed in the same room as their elders—create a polymorphous sexuality that mocks our reductive categories of sexual identity. Although homosexuality may be vilified in macho settings, everyone knows that this is a policy for the surface and that many of the participants also have developed fully articulated same-sex sidelines, partly for survival and subsequently for pleasure. In the Anglo-Saxon world, with its heritage of philosophical materialism, the surface claims an exact match with what goes on underneath. But this is not so in the culture of poverty, where the bravado of appearances is one thing and off-the-record experiences and feelings are another. A man's got to have an image, but he must not become a slave to it.

The sophisticated interplay between surface realities and inner realities in underclass life is in sharp contrast to the reductive tendencies of class-prejudiced identity politics, with its formula of actions equaling identity. And the controversies of the closet and outing—two favorites of gay politics—collapse into superficiality in the context of the street. In Times Square I met many married men who were not homosexual but who had a passion for transvestites. Sometimes they even enjoyed being the passive partner with someone who had both a penis and a female image (breasts, et cetera). But they would have been repulsed by the idea of having sex with anyone who looked like a man. They simply were not gay.

A hustler I knew did it less for the money than for isolated heightened experiences in which he could lose himself sucking cock while he focused on a straight porno film playing in the background. During these fugue states, I could sense his fantasies flow in shifting, disembodied identifications first with the man in the film, then the woman, then with me, and then with himself as someone with a cock in his mouth. He was intensely attracted to women and had a wife but was probably capable of a whole pattern of relationships with males on a deeply felt level. Still, he preferred to accumulate homosexual feelings until they spilled out in isolated erotic episodes. If he'd been "outed"—if he'd been forced to articulate all the libido he'd accumulated around the ritualistic episodes of cock-sucking into something rational and community-minded—he probably would have lost his complicated erotic relationships with the women and men in his life. There are sexual impulses that are too fragmented to base an entire sociological identity upon. To brand them simply as "closeted" is intolerant and presumptuous.

If one must find identity in homosexuality, then all that really remains are some disturbing physical and social factors: Homosexuals can't make babies with each other, and nonproduction of a family automatically sets one outside the mainstream. In his erotic activity, the homosexual is likely to encounter other outsiders, such as bisexuals. In a country that functions upon the assumptions of fixed identities, bisexuals are likely to lead unconventional lives that partake of other marginalized populations. For example, there is a heavy incidence of bisexuality in the world of drug users and in the culture of poverty. This means that the homosexual, who will encounter bisexuals, is likely to interact occasionally with these populations at risk. Because of its nonbreeding status and its association with marginality, homosexuality is one ideal position from which to challenge the conventional structures of society. It could again serve as the starting point for a new class-oriented counterculture mentality.

Today, identity politics is one of many facets of the middle-class mentality that has absorbed some marginals and worked to sever the old, fertile connections among bohemia, the culture of poverty, and the avant-garde. Our current politics spends a lot of time fearfully discussing the uncontrollability of libidinal behavior and deconstructing aestheticism while it continues to neglect the embarrassing subject of class. Concurrently, it has become the voice of one ruling class—the homogenized suburban bourgeoisie. For the liberal, there are many ironies in the new politics; among them is the following: about those we liberals have been taught not to vilify— the poor—there is now no language to speak about at all.

Lack of class-consciousness is America's glaring, unspoken sin. There has been no voice to discuss class since the thirties, when the working class was at stake and before America became a service economy. Whether a particular voice of today's "multiculturalism" has a black face, a woman's face, a gay face, or a working-class face is now beside the point. All speak the language of the well fed.

The denaturing of class issues was helped along by deconstructionist specialists in the universities, who dismantled politically offensive canonical texts and approved of or condemned behavior without anthropological reference to the intrinsic values of the people from which it sprang. The devaluation of some of the more sociologically authentic, sensual, deranged, and aesthetic literary texts we have began with the aim of liberation from imposed norms and ended up with the boiler-plating of the burgeoning id, which is by definition obscene and aggressive, but which is the fount of energy for the creative artist. When it comes to discussing outsider culture, academics have invented distanced cynical terms like "performance" or "transgression." Giving voice to the reality of poverty in all its lustiness, energy, and degradation has become taboo, and it is actually considered a slight to a poor person's integrity to tell the reality of his cultural experiences.

For the gelded inhabitant of today's so-called counterculture, I see only one possible action in the face of a voiceless, unacknowledged underclass and a strangulated middle class. That is a mental coalition between the disaffected bohemian and the culture of poverty. Street people speak of appetites and aggressions that artistic middle-class people can help them articulate. But first it must be admitted that in underclass life, identity cannot be conveniently sifted out and defined. Hunger, homelessness, or drug addiction always take precedence. On the street, everybody is a "nigger." And there is a certain depth of need or disorganization at which a person will stick it in anybody or let anyone at all stick it in.

These chaotic energies are the "sickness" that Nordau thought the avant-garde artists of his time had been infected with. And it was from this swamp of urban libido that some of the last century's richest artistic creations were to flower. The same alchemy is possible in this new century, but more so, for never before has the dichotomy of middle-class decency and urban degeneration been more skewed.